Please pray for me.

Patrick Madrid

SURPRISED BY LIFE

SURPRISED BY LIFE

10 CONVERTS EXPLAIN HOW CATHOLIC TEACHINGS ON LIFE LED THEM TO THE CHURCH

Edited by Patrick Madrid

SOPHIA INSTITUTE PRESS
Manchester, New Hampshire

Sophia Institute Press
Box 5284, Manchester, NH 03108
1-800-888-9344

www.SophiaInstitute.com

Sophia Institute Press® is a registered trademark of Sophia Institute.

Library of Congress Cataloging-in-Publication Data

Names: Madrid, Patrick, 1960- editor.

Title: Surprised by life : 9 converts explain how Catholic teachings on life led them to the church / edited by Patrick Madrid.

Description: Manchester, New Hampshire : Sophia Institute Press, 2017.

Identifiers: LCCN 2017011064 | ISBN 9781622823734 (pbk. : alk. paper)

Subjects: LCSH: Catholic converts — Biography. | Abortion — Religious aspects — Catholic Church.

Classification: LCC BX4668.A1 S86 2017 | DDC 248.2/420922 [B] — dc23 LC record available at https://lccn.loc.gov/2017011064

First printing

Dedicated with gratitude and all my love to Nancy—my wife of thirty-six years, mother of our eleven children, and grandmother of our twenty-one grandchildren (so far). You, my dear, have taught me more than you realize about the joys and blessings of being surprised by life.

CONTENTS

INTRODUCTION

PATRICK MADRID

Twenty-three years ago, *Surprised by Truth*, the first volume in my "Surprised By" series of conversion-story books debuted, followed in 2000 by *Surprised by Truth 2* and in 2002 by *Surprised by Truth 3*. In those days, the hot-ticket items among Catholic readers were apologetics-heavy, first-person stories of conversion to the Catholic Church—the more biblical and historical, the better.

Two of the elements that have made the "Surprised By" testimonies stand out from other conversion stories are their compelling honesty about doctrinal struggles and their candid accounts of the often enormous obstacles these converts strove to surmount along their way into the Catholic Church.

Numerous readers of these books have told me how profoundly these testimonies affected them, speaking directly to their hearts, catching them by surprise, breaking down their prejudices, strengthening their convictions, answering their objections, dispelling falsehoods and half-truths, gladdening their hearts, and changing their lives in many other ways.

God has used these "Surprised By" testimonies to move their readers in mysterious ways, shining His healing rays of grace into those hard-to-reach, often hidden, and humanly inaccessible redoubts of the human heart in which we often seek shelter from the truth.

Jesus promised that we shall know the truth and the truth will set us free. Often, God uses heartfelt personal testimonies like keys to open the prison cells of our minds. The previously locked door swings open, the truth enters in, and another captive heart is set free. As the teachings and miracles of Jesus demonstrate so often in the Gospels, many of us are utterly unaware that we even need to be set free!

A quarter century and half a million copies later (including foreign and foreign-language editions) comes the fourth volume in the "Surprised By" series—*Surprised by Life*. Here are ten new personal testimonies that go beyond scriptural, historical, and doctrinal apologetics and deep into the tumultuous territory of life issues, including the tragic and sudden loss of a young-adult child, the pain of miscarriage, abortion, contraception, hedonism, promiscuity, drug and alcohol abuse, and even prostitution. None of these testimonies of God's forgiveness and healing love are titillating or salacious, but all are raw and honest, in ways reminiscent of St. Augustine's raw and honest, but never titillating, *Confessions*.

Each of these testimonies brims with the *real-life* life issues faced today by many folks, including persons we love and even those in our families.

As you turn the page and enter into these captivating human dramas—tragedy and triumph, trial and error, hitting rock bottom and rising above—my prayer is that, like these remarkable men and women, you, too, will be surprised by life, surprised by truth, and surprised by God's boundless grace and love.

PATRICK MADRID is a lifelong Catholic. He hosts the popular daily *Patrick Madrid Show* on Immaculate Heart/ Relevant Radio (Monday through Friday, 6:00 to 9:00 a.m. Pacific, ihradio.com/patrick). Before launching that show, he hosted *Right Here, Right Now*, broadcast on approximately 350 AM and FM stations across the United States as well as on Sirius Satellite Radio and globally via shortwave. He is a frequent guest and occasional guest host on the *Catholic Answers Live* radio program.

Patrick has authored or edited twenty-five books on Catholic themes, including *Life Lessons: Fifty Things I Learned in My First Fifty Years, Why Be Catholic?, Search and Rescue, Does the Bible Really Say That?* and the acclaimed *Surprised by Truth* series.

Commenting publicly on the effectiveness of Patrick's approach to apologetics, the late Cardinal Edward Egan said, "How do you bring a friend or relative back into the Church? First you pray. Then, you follow Patrick Madrid's advice in *Search and Rescue*."

Patrick worked at Catholic Answers for eight years, where he served as vice president. A veteran of a dozen formal, public debates with Protestant ministers, Mormon leaders, and other non-Catholic spokesmen, Patrick has presented countless seminars on Catholic themes, in English and in Spanish, at parishes, universities, and conferences across the United States and around the world.

For some thirty years, Patrick has published numerous popular articles on Scripture, Church history, patristics, apologetics, and evangelization in various Catholic and Protestant periodicals, and he has contributed scholarly articles on apologetics to the *New Catholic Encyclopedia*. He earned a bachelor of science in business at the University of Phoenix, as well as a B.Phil. in philosophy and a master's in dogmatic theology at the Pontifical College Josephinum (Columbus, Ohio).

Patrick has served as an adjunct professor of theology at Franciscan University of Steubenville and currently teaches as an adjunct professor of theology in the graduate theology program at Holy Apostles College and Seminary in Cromwell, Connecticut (holyapostles.edu/patrick).

Married for thirty-six years, Patrick and his wife, Nancy, have been blessed by the Lord with eleven children and twenty-one grandchildren (so far).

PATRICKMADRID.COM

IHRADIO.COM/PATRICK

HOLYAPOSTLES.EDU/PATRICK

TWITTER: @PATRICKMADRID

SURPRISED BY LIFE

AUNT AMY SAVES MY BABY

HEATHER SCHIEDER

I am the daughter of hardworking parents. My father is an immigrant from Cairo, Egypt, who moved to Buffalo, New York, learned the language, and worked hard to be a good citizen. He succeeded.

My mom, who is of Irish and English descent, was born and raised here in America. After she and my father married and began having children, she went back to school and became a nurse.

When I was a high school freshman, my mom gave me a book that described—in detail—what happens during an abortion. I quickly read that thing from cover to cover, and I was completely shocked and sickened.

My parents raised us Maronite Catholic. We went to church every Sunday. I didn't like church all that much. I didn't speak

Arabic like most of the other children my age, so I felt like an outsider. I made my sacraments but didn't have a relationship with God at all.

I loved making people laugh. I learned very early that being funny could protect my sensitive heart and could help me anytime I felt vulnerable. As an adult, I'm still very much this way, though I've learned since then that vulnerability is not weakness, but strength. I still love making people laugh, but I also love connecting with others through a mutual sharing of our stories, vulnerability, and honesty.

We lived in a small, mostly white town. Not everyone accepted our family, with a white mom and a Middle Eastern dad. Sometimes I was made fun of and called racist names. It hurt me. From a young age, I empathized with those who suffered injustice, and once I knew the truth about abortion, it was only natural that I would feel empathy for the unborn, too — so much so that when my ninth-grade English teacher assigned my class an oral report on a controversial issue, I chose abortion.

My position?

Pro-life.

I remember the day I stood in front of my class. I was never known for being serious. I enjoyed annoying my teachers by asking them silly questions, especially my French teacher. The day I got him mad enough to chase me breathlessly around the classroom was the happiest day of my high school experience. I was a cross between Darlene on *Roseanne* and Beavis of *Beavis and Butthead*.

But that day in front of my class, I was dead serious. I told my class everything I had learned about what really happens during an abortion. By the time I was done there was palpable tension in the room. Some students were touched by what they had heard. Others, though, were furious.

AUNT AMY SAVES MY BABY

It was scary to face that, but I did it because I was convinced that what I said was true.

Conviction might be easy when you're standing behind a pulpit or a lectern; it's harder when you have to practice what you preach.

Fast-forward two years. I was a moody, difficult teenager, and I despised the fact that my parents were strict. After a particularly difficult time, I made a hasty decision to run away from home. I packed my things and went to a homeless shelter for teens. The place seemed okay at first, but then I found that the other teens there were like experienced thugs and I was a silly little suburban girl trying hard to look tough.

I had never had sex or done drugs before, but the day I arrived at the shelter, a young, muscular male counselor handed me a huge bag filled with things of different colors that I mistakenly thought were balloons. "Gosh, this place is fun!" I thought. "Look at all those balloons! There's like a hundred of them!" Wrong! The guy told me they were condoms.

"Oh!" I said. "Well, the thing is, I don't really need these things."

"What do you mean?" he asked.

"Um ... I mean, I don't do that ... stuff."

In a condescending voice, he told me that I did indeed need those things. I was embarrassed and grossed out that some older guy was cornering me about my nonexistent sex life. It felt wildly inappropriate for him to do that, and I didn't know how to respond properly. It made me feel ashamed, as if I had somehow brought this upon myself. I was insulted and angry. How dare he judge me without even knowing me! He seemed convinced that I would need the entire bag.

As it turned out, he was correct.

That night, as all the residents ran around like a pack of wild dogs with barely any supervision, I came up with a creative way to use the condoms. I set to work immediately, covering every doorknob, faucet, and showerhead with brightly colored condoms. I was in full party-planning mode and felt just like a young, crafty Martha Stewart. This project had it all: pops of color, strategic placement, repurposing something in a useful, earth-friendly way: it was like something straight off Pinterest.

The same counselor who insisted I'd needed the whole bag tried to turn one of the newly updated doorknobs, and when his hand slipped off (lubricated!), he was furious. More joy for me! The showerheads bursting in the bathrooms the next morning sent him into even greater fury, and I was thrilled because I had had the last laugh. I felt like a champion! I still think it's hilarious.

After my little stint at the shelter, I stayed with a friend and her family and resumed going to high school, where, between my failing grades and my foolish behavior, I continued to be a problem. I had an English teacher who believed in me, and I enjoyed creative writing. But I didn't believe in myself and had no idea what I was doing with my life: I had no direction, no real goals, and no belief that I could accomplish anything good.

When my friend's family moved to another district, I had to find a new place to live. The year before, I had had a religious education teacher at our parish who was related to me through marriage. We called her "Aunt Amy." She had just had a reversion back to the Faith, and I really liked her and enjoyed her class. She had a huge heart and a charismatic personality, and on the last day of class she told us that if ever we needed help or wanted to talk, we could come and find her at the restaurant she owned in North Buffalo. It was a tiny restaurant with delicious food, and it catered mainly to college students.

So I visited Aunt Amy at her restaurant, told her my situation, and asked her if I could come to live with her. After I made it clear to her that I was desperate, she agreed. She talked with my mom, and I went to live with her.

The house wasn't huge, but it was a nice home and very well cared for. There was beautiful woodwork, the dining room was lovely, and the living room was large with a fireplace and a sectional sofa positioned in front of it. It was a relaxing, cozy space where you'd want to curl up with a good book or watch one of the many movies in Amy's video library.

There was also a den that I think must have been at one time an efficient office space. Following Amy's enthusiastic reversion to the Faith, she had stripped it down and moved in hundreds of statues of Jesus and His Mother, plus almost every saint you can imagine, all crammed close together, each of their faces either grimly serious or extremely elated. There was no middle ground. To be honest, this room scared me, and I avoided it at all costs.

One time I got stuck there for a few minutes. With all the lit candles, the room was as hot as an oven, and I felt like fainting. It was like being in a tiny sauna with a million antique dolls, their glass eyes honing in on you, and only you, searing into your soul and accusing you of that little third-grade sin you conveniently forgot to confess: the time you stole all the candies from your teacher's candy dish, one at a time, as you walked out of class each day. No one else remembered this except for you — you and God and all His little porcelain friends with the haunting expressions, staring at you now in this tiny suffocating room.

The way I felt about that room was the way I felt about God, as some strict, merciless tyrant in the sky with a kind of vaguely annoying Peeping Tom vibe. When I sinned, I imagined Him peeking at me and tsk-tsk-tsking away at me from His royal perch in the clouds. It was really irritating that He was always watching me, like a fly buzzing around over my dinner plate.

You see, I didn't know God is a loving Father. I knew Him only as someone who saw me as I believed I really was: a bad person with zero worth.

Every Sunday, Amy invited me to go to Mass; and every Sunday I snuggled deeper under the covers and called out, "No, thanks" in a groggy voice. She never forced me to go, but she always invited me. She knew that forcing me would likely have had the opposite of the desired effect and that I'd wind up separating myself from God even more.

So she never shamed me for not going to Mass. Instead, she did what Jesus would do: she simply loved me. She laughed at my stupid jokes. She treated me as if I were her daughter. She built me up by complimenting me on my strengths. And she told me that God loved me always, no matter what.

There was her best friend, her best friend's two kids, and a middle-aged cousin. The kids were both around my age and were always getting into trouble and smoking a lot of pot. I started smoking with them. This was a bad idea: pot seemed instantly to transform me from a relatively normal teenager into a doddering old man. For example, one time I smoked at a friend's house, and although I wasn't far from home, it took me close to an hour to get there, and I couldn't figure out why. It was freezing outside, too. As my buzz began to wear off, I realized that I had been walking around the same city block over and over, at least six times.

In those days, I liked boys who were always in trouble — not prank-playing trouble but dropout, drug-dealer trouble.

I didn't think, "Gosh, I'd really love to date someone with a serious criminal record!" I just didn't know how to relate to normal guys my own age. I was drawn to ones who were really mean and treated me badly. I didn't believe that I had a shot at any guys who were responsible and good because I wasn't responsible myself and I didn't consider myself to be good.

When a guy leaned out of his car window and said, "Pssst! Yo girl! What's yo name?" I believed he really liked me. That's how confused I was.

One day my friend and I visited her boyfriend, who lived in a bad neighborhood. He was drunk and was hanging out with another guy who was also drinking. I had no idea who the other guy was, but he was cute and seemed sad and lonely. I quickly got involved with him. Although we never even went out on a single date, we soon became intimate. I was needy, naïve, and insecure, and he was a total player who used me. I couldn't see it at the time. We called each other boyfriend and girlfriend, but he was cheating on me all the time.

Soon, Aunt Amy's house came to be filled with all kinds of people—kinds I had never encountered before: drug addicts, alcoholics, prostitutes, and folks with mental illness. There was a crack-addicted lesbian couple who slept on the sectional and constantly bickered. There was a man who had been kicked out of his home by his wife because he wouldn't stop drinking. Every day he would call her repeatedly on the phone, wailing "LENOOOORE!!! LENOOOORE!!!" over and over again until you couldn't even think straight and everyone yelled at him to shut up.

My new housemates were way older than me and had faced things I couldn't even imagine facing. There was the lesbian addict, who had lived a life of abuse as a child. Her own mother was so afraid of her getting pregnant that she crushed birth-control pills and sneaked them into her daughter's food. Only the neighborhood prostitute had been consistently kind to her. One day, when she was a little girl playing outside, she said hello to her friend the prostitute. The next moment she watched that same prostitute get shot in the head, right in front of her.

Living together under one roof, we were encouraged to be like family to each other, and that's what we became. I was everyone's funny and annoying little sister, and I could make them laugh. I also had a special knack for frustrating them because I was lazy and selfish and didn't clean up after myself. They were quick to inform me, and in not so many kind words, that they were not my parents or my personal slaves. It was exactly the kind of kick in the butt that I needed.

The men and women who lived in that house were truly like older siblings to me. They stuck up for me if they saw anyone messing with me; they taught me to cook; they yelled at me when I dropped out of school. One of them yelled at me so bad that I had to move into a separate apartment for a while. I found out later that she had been tough on me because she knew I was smart and it pained her that I was throwing it all away. I didn't know it at the time, but she was illiterate and could barely write her own name. She didn't want to see me end up like her.

I didn't really have friends my own age anymore, so the people I lived with became my friends. I was a stranger to my family, so these troubled folks became my family. Despite their brokenness, they truly tried to be a good influence on me. They didn't do drugs around me or invite me to do drugs; and they busted me when I tried to sneak around with my boyfriend.

They even brought me with them to their Narcotics Anonymous meetings. I was bored and had nothing else to do anyway, and those meetings were entertaining in the very best way. We would listen to people share their stories, and believe it or not, some of the best storytellers, comedians, and poets in the world are found in those meetings. Suffering can do that to a person.

Usually, we would laugh like crazy, cry like babies, and shout, "Amen!" all in the same night. It was amazing to see honest, humble people opening up about the most heart-wrenching moments and admitting the deepest shame. For me, it was refreshing. It inspired me and taught me a lot about character and life.

All this time I was still involved with my boyfriend. Then one day he disappeared, just about the same time that I started feeling sick. I soon realized I was pregnant.

I was scared.

I didn't know what to do.

I completely freaked out. If I could've climbed out of my own body and run for the hills, I would have. I was in a constant state of panic. My biggest fear was having my parents find out about it and facing their reaction. I literally wanted to die.

I confided in one of the other women in the house. She had become like an older sister to me. She told me that she had had three abortions and she knew where I could get one.

That ninth-grade project I had done on the truths of abortion seemed like a lifetime ago. Where was the girl who had felt that sense of injustice, who wanted to stand up for those whom no one would stand up for?

Well, she was basically hunkered down and having a panic attack. You see, this wasn't a random girl in some book or a character in a movie. This wasn't the set of the *Ricki Lake Show*. This was my actual life: the girl in crisis was me. I was frantic and desperate and more afraid than I had ever been in my life.

I called the clinic and made the appointment.

It was a Friday when I called, and they scheduled me for the upcoming Monday. I was scared, but relieved. One thought filled my mind: "Let me get through the next two days really fast and then I can get this whole thing over on Monday." I didn't ever stop to consider that a person was growing inside me. Instead, what I was thinking and feeling was "Oh *expletive*, I'm in trouble. I need to get out of this before they find out."

I was like a wild-eyed, frightened animal. I felt as if I had committed some horrible crime and was about to lose my life. It wasn't the thought of being a mom that scared me. It was my fear of telling any authority in my life that I had gotten pregnant. I was ashamed and fearful of their condemnation. That was my worst nightmare. I would do anything, anything, to avoid it.

The next day, my aunt cooked a big dinner for all of us at the house. This was a perfect distraction. Food! Delicious food!

I don't remember any of the guys being at the dinner, just all the ladies. I had been so excited about this dinner because it was my favorite — pasta and sauce. Finally, we all sat down around the big dining-room table. We said Grace, and as I started to dig in, I suddenly felt as if I would throw up.

Reality set back in as I was reminded of my situation, and I asked to be excused from the table. I went upstairs to my bedroom and sat on my bed with my arms wrapped around my stomach. I tried not to get sick, and my heart raced with fear as I allowed myself to think about why I was feeling sick. I grew afraid of going to that Monday appointment. I wished I could tell someone besides the woman I had told. I wished I could tell Aunt Amy.

Fortunately, at that same moment, she had a sneaking feeling that something was up with me and suspected what it might be. Once I was safely upstairs, she looked around at the remaining women at the table, and said, "Let me ask you all a question. Is Heather pregnant?" They all avoided eye contact with her and looked down at their plates. No one wanted to tell on me, but they didn't want to lie, either. The general thought was something like "I ain't saying nothin'."

What happened next was a game changer. It's one of the single most important things that has ever happened in my life, and if you are someone who wants to help stop abortion, then I ask you to pay close attention. Because it was all about the way my aunt approached me. It was all about the way she walked in.

There I was, rocking on my bed, feeling lost and afraid and hopeless. I heard someone climbing the stairs, and I swore under my breath. *Crap*.

It was Aunt Amy.

I heard a gentle, respectful knock on my bedroom door. In a kind voice, she said, "Can I come in?"

That moment right there helped me to let my guard down. Instead of tensing up and putting on an act, I allowed myself to become transparent. I didn't try to hide the fear in my eyes or make up some excuse about how I must have the flu or something. I didn't say anything.

She asked me, "Heather, honey … are you pregnant?"

I burst out crying.

I had been carrying all this fear and dread inside and trying so hard to ignore my feelings that it was a huge relief to cry about it. I was relieved that I didn't have to be the one to say anything. Hearing the compassion in her voice and her honest-to-goodness concern for me made me feel safe enough to tell the truth. So that's what I did. In fact, I immediately began sobbing and cried out, "I don't want to have an abortion!"

AUNT AMY SAVES MY BABY

I hadn't let myself really confront the abortion question until that moment when I felt safe, but I think subconsciously it was there all along. That's part of the reason I had to shut everything out in my head all weekend, because I probably knew that if I thought about it too much, I would cancel the abortion.

Can you really call that kind of fear freedom?

Is that kind of fear what's truly best for a vulnerable woman — that she should have to shut her eyes and mind and heart so she will be able to kill her baby?

To make that decision, she has to silence every ounce of her humanity. That just doesn't seem the right way to make a genuinely healthy choice. That's fear and anxiety and all other kinds of unseen pressures pushing her to choose abortion, which leaves countless women hurting and aching and longing for the chance to go back and make a different choice from the one they were rushed into making.

I was lucky.

I'm aware of this.

I was lucky that someone was able to be "wise as a serpent and gentle as a dove," as Christ instructed His followers to be in Matthew 10:16.

If you have had an abortion, I want to tell you how very sorry I am. I'm sorry that there wasn't an Aunt Amy there for you. I'm sorry that people let you down. I'm sorry that you weren't surrounded with true support, the kind that does the real work of true love and sacrifice. And I hope you know that there's nothing about me that's more special or deserving than you.

I was simply lucky.

When I sobbed out the words, "I don't want to have an abortion!" Amy's immediate response was, "Honey! I would never want you to have an abortion! I will help you. We will be there for you and for the baby. We're going to buy you diapers and clothes and a crib and everything you need."

It was actually pretty hilarious: she was joyfully and frantically rattling off an entire baby-essentials list to me, and I was sobbing and coming to grips with the fact that this was happening. I sobbed because I was so relieved and a weight had been lifted off my shoulders. I sobbed because I finally let myself cry. I sobbed because this crazy lady was telling me she would buy me formula and I had no idea what she was even talking about.

But it was all good.

I was still afraid to tell my parents, but it was all good. And I began to believe that, somehow, it would be okay.

I had to face a lot of things.

For one, when I finally told my baby's daddy about the pregnancy, he was not on board. He demanded that I have an abortion. Luckily, I had already received enough support to stand firm in my decision to keep my baby. But I was heartbroken over his response and over the fact that he had already moved on with another girl.

AUNT AMY SAVES MY BABY

I had to face the fact that people would look at me differently, and some of them would scorn me and treat me like a loser. This included some of the employees at Aunt Amy's restaurant. I had to face family members who were scandalized and bitterly disappointed in me. It was difficult, and I had a hard time with it. But eventually it made me into a stronger person.

Thankfully, I had enough people to love me through that time, and I soon discovered that two other women who lived in the house were also pregnant. It was like a maternity home!

One of the pregnant women was a heroin addict. She tried to stop using but didn't succeed. One day, when she was a little more than halfway through her pregnancy, she delivered her baby into a toilet at the house. I wasn't home when it happened, but when I got home, one of the guys was freaking out and saying, "The baby was moving in there! It was paddling its hands in the water, I swear!" I had no clue what he was talking about.

The ambulance had been there and taken the mom to the hospital, so we headed straight there. She was in a hospital room and had the baby with her. He was the same gestational age as my baby. He was not doing well, but he was alive.

She was holding him against her bare chest, and it was the most heartbreaking thing to see that poor baby struggling and to witness the raw sorrow and emotion of his mother. She asked me if I'd like to hold him, and I said yes.

He was long and skinny, with ten perfect fingers and toes and a beautiful little face. His eyes were sealed shut, unable to open yet at this stage of development. I laid him across my lap and watched him in complete awe. This was a person—a living, breathing, real, live human being. He was a little bit scary to look at, being so fragile and not fully developed, but he was clearly a baby. And he truly was beautiful.

We stayed there all day, and he didn't live very long. He died the next morning. The nurses and doctors said there was nothing they could do. But they were very kind, caring, and respectful.

A lot of people might say that that baby's life was a mistake or a waste, but I don't believe that at all. He certainly wasn't carried in the best of circumstances, and he deserved much better. But in those last days of his life, he was cherished.

He wasn't simply a lesson or some prop for the pro-life movement, either. He was a child with dignity, and he was surrounded by love. He was held lovingly during every moment of his earthly life. As he rested upon his mother's breast, he received that love and gave that love right back to her. All of us there with him — doctors and nurses included — were deeply touched by that baby, just by being near him. There was so much love in that room, and it moved our hearts, like a little kiss from heaven.

While I was pregnant, my aunt Amy bought some church property from the diocese and started a Catholic missionary community whose primary work was to help the poor. I moved there along with her, and so did a bunch of other people. I still didn't ever go to Mass, but one day she took me to Adoration of the Blessed Sacrament and told me just to tell Jesus whatever was in my heart — just to talk to Him as if He was my friend.

I did, and I felt comforted.

AUNT AMY SAVES MY BABY

A group of men and women from the local pro-life chapter threw a baby shower for me and for one of the other moms. It was amazing. They gave each of us so many beautiful baby things, things that we never could have afforded. Not only that: the people who attended were genuinely kind and happy for us. They were just the sweetest people, folks who really cared. They had a huge cake and lots of food, and there was even a priest there who prayed over us and gave us a blessing.

Finally, November came along, and I gave birth to a gorgeous little baby boy named Joseph. I distinctly remember the moment when I picked him up and he made the tiniest little baby sounds, his legs curled up beneath him. I fell completely in love with him in that moment. It was so intense and life changing, and I can still go back and feel what I felt in that moment. If my heart could have spoken what it felt then, it would have said "You are mine. You are mine."

Being a new mom was not easy. I had a lot of help, a beautiful room for my baby, and everything I needed, but I was still overwhelmed and stressed out. I had a hard time making the necessary sacrifices for my baby.

Despite the fact that I loved him fiercely, I made many mistakes along the way. I went right into a relationship with another guy, and although he genuinely cared about me and my baby, he was a serious drug addict who sometimes became physically abusive. Also, our relationship was not a chaste one. This relationship went on for about a year.

I got my son baptized and started going back to church, but I wasn't really into it. I just went along because everyone else did, and because my boyfriend would join us and that made me feel as if I had a real family.

But God always finds a way to reel you in when you're lost. The people in that parish community were a family to me, and they spoke of God's love for me and my baby. There were volunteers who visited; some of them were grandmothers already. One of them even lived with my son and me in a community house for a few years. She helped me care for him, and he called her "Granny." To this day, she and her family have a special place in our lives.

There was a volunteer named Barb who would talk and laugh with me, listen when I was down, and encourage me to get back up and do the right thing. There were so many women and men who spoke hope to me when I had none. Little by little, my heart began to change without my even realizing it.

In the fall of 1995, when my son was just about to turn a year old, I was invited to go with the mission community to New York City for a special Mass. I was excited about the chance to visit the city! I mean, it was for Pope John Paul II's Mass in Central Park, which sounded downright boring to me, but I was willing to suffer through it to go on the trip.

I hated going to church. What was the point? Besides, wasn't the pope sort of like a dictator anyway? He was probably going to yell at us or at least give us Americans a stern talking to for our sinful behavior.

We rode one of the buses that the diocese had provided. It was fun, and we laughed a lot. When we finally arrived, I was tired. We found a spot in the park. It was very loud there, but I pulled my hood up over my head and thought to myself, "Good. Now I can just sit here on the grass and fall asleep until this thing is over."

I was almost completely asleep, my head in my hands, when I heard a voice cry out, "America!! Do not be afraid to stand up for life." I was jerked out of my sleep. I wondered who was saying that. I stood right up and realized it was the pope! And as he continued talking, I felt something come over me. This guy didn't sound harsh at all. In fact, he sounded like a loving father. I wasn't used to that.

I didn't think of God as being that way at all. I was mesmerized. As he talked about standing up for life and being courageous, I did something I hardly ever did: I began to weep—not because I was afraid or in trouble, but because I felt consoled and loved. And I felt so uplifted by the pope's words. You see, I had always felt like such a complete loser, but there was one thing I was proud of—one thing I knew I had done right: I had chosen life for my little son.

As I stood there crying, I watched crowds of people my own age cheering for the pope and crying out, "John Paul 2, we love you!" over and over again. They looked like people I could relate to, people I'd choose to be friends with, and they were having so much fun. They were so alive! And so filled with joy.

When it came time to receive the Eucharist, I had a major realization: I was not in a state of grace. My sins were separating me from God, from receiving the Body and Blood of Christ, and I felt a deep sense of sorrow. I felt like I was missing out on something so huge.

And I was. I was missing out on God Himself.

That was the beginning of a very real conversion. That was the moment when God began truly to draw me back to the Church.

It was a process and did not happen overnight, but it did happen. I struggled with chastity most of all. That was the toughest part, honestly. But little by little, I started coming back. I went to confession, usually once a week. It was embarrassing sometimes, but the priest was never scandalized. The more I went to confession, the more I refrained from those same embarrassing sins that brought me such misery and chipped away at my sense of self-worth.

God brought so much healing into my life.

He helped me to become a better mother. He reunited me with my parents and my siblings. He helped me to gain the confidence I needed to get my GED and go to college for a few years. He helped me to leave unhealthy relationships behind and to begin to recognize my worth.

None of that probably would ever have happened if it weren't for that moment when my aunt Amy walked into my bedroom with kindness and gentle concern. Simply put, my son would not be here if it weren't for her and the way she approached me.

I spent many years being zealous about my Faith and aggressively pro-life. I drew my sword in many a Facebook battle and came out bloodied and beaten, but more often feeling victorious due to some snarky remark I made or some well-delivered fact. I've felt the virtual pats on the back from my own echo chamber. Many times, I've said things that hurt others deeply.

As a result, here's what I've learned.

Mean-spirited snark, acting like a condescending know-it-all, and having the last word will not make a lasting, positive difference in our culture. It doesn't change hearts—in fact, it does the exact opposite—and hearts are what need to be changed if we want to see a true culture of life. I've also learned that it takes a lot more than scientific facts and philosophical arguments to get through to others. Pure reason is not enough. How we speak to people, how we treat them, means an awful lot. If our pro-life witness consists of arguing people to death through a computer screen instead of getting outside our comfort zone and being a loving, kind human being, then we still don't get what it means to be truly pro-life.

The battle for the unborn, for life versus death, begins and ends in the human heart. But our love has to be real and not contrived. That doesn't mean we need to feel lovey-dovey feelings all the time, because we know that's not real love anyway, but it does mean that love, not winning, is our goal.

We must seek to understand and empathize with those who don't agree with us. We must be very careful with our speech, especially when speaking about women in crisis pregnancies, including those who have chosen abortion. We have to speak with compassion and kindness and remember that post-abortive women are often suffering silently all around us, listening to and reading what we say. Their babies were not the only victims at the abortion clinic. They were victims, too, and they can't go back and undo what has been done.

I think back to that day in my bedroom when I was in a state of panic, and how Aunt Amy's words and tone made the difference between life and death for my unborn son. I pray that I can be like that in every area of my life. That's not easy for this Irish Middle Eastern woman, but I'm working on it.

For many years after my last bad relationship I took a break from dating. I lived and worked as a missionary for several years when my son was growing up, and sometimes I lost heart and thought that maybe I was too damaged ever to be able to get married and have a family. Thankfully, I was wrong.

I've been married now for over ten years to a good man who is truly my best friend. My little Joey grew up to be a handsome, hardworking, kind, and funny young man of whom I am very proud. My husband, Dan, legally adopted him after we were married, and Joey now has five younger siblings. One of them is in heaven now, a baby girl whom we lost to miscarriage about a month ago.

We have a great life. It's not a perfect life, of course. Only heaven is perfect. But we try our best and practice our Catholic Faith. I still love to make people laugh, and I love to have fun. Over the last few years, the gifts of writing and creating art that I loved as a child have resurfaced in my life. I'm always learning and growing as a person.

My life is proof that our God is merciful and that His Church is a refuge and a "hospital for sinners," as Pope Francis often says. It is a place where life is celebrated and embraced.

If you are in the same place I was, please don't lose hope. God has a good plan for your life! Even if you've made mistakes as I did, even if you had an abortion, God has never stopped loving you. And His good plans for your life have not been made impossible by anything you've done.

Our God makes everything new. He waits for us in the sacraments. He gives us another chance. "His mercies are new every morning." He wants to bring healing into our lives so that we can be the people we are truly meant to be.

Christ said to St. Faustina, "The greater the sinner, the greater the right he has to My mercy" (*Diary* 723). So have great trust in the heart of Jesus, who is kind and loving and waiting for us with great joy. There is nothing beyond Him, and you are meant to play a part in His life, a part that can be played only by you.

HEATHER SCHIEDER lives outside Buffalo, New York, and is a Catholic writer, speaker, artisan, wannabe comedian, and the proud winner of the Most Caffeinated Mother in America contest. She and her husband, Dan, a man who is swiftly approaching sainthood, are the parents of five beautiful, smiley kids, plus one more in heaven.

HEATHERSCHIEDER@GMAIL.COM

WWW.MAMAKNOWSHONEYCHILD.COM

INSTAGRAM: @HONEYCHILDFOREST

CALL GIRL TO CATHOLIC

ANNEMARIE SCHREIBER

My parents divorced when I was a toddler. Afterward, they batted me to and fro like a hockey puck.

One would strap a psychological bomb to me before hurling me headlong toward the other. For example, my father would send me home from summer vacation with a boyish haircut, knowing that my mom had spent the entire year growing my hair out; and mom would doll me up in gaudy clothes sure to offend my dad's snobbish sensibilities. The result? Each greeted me with a scowl when I returned from the other.

My father was a fallen-away Catholic. He never had me baptized, but he did take me to Mass once when I was seven—I don't remember why. I do recall being thrilled. As we were walking across the parking lot afterward, I asked him if we could start going to Mass every Sunday. He gave me the queerest raised-eyebrow look and asked, "Why on earth would you want to do that?" Predictably, he never honored my request.

That episode is emblematic of our relationship throughout my childhood. I felt I was always seeking his affection and attention, and being misunderstood, put off, or denied outright. No matter how intensely I expressed my love for him, or how impressive my achievements, he seemed perpetually disinterested. In the movie of my father's life, my scenes always wound up on the cutting-room floor.

My mother was a party girl with an insatiable thirst for brutal men, booze, and cocaine. She was a master manipulator who, my grandmother often said, could sell bedsheets to a Bedouin.

She proved it when my dad sued for custody. She employed all sorts of dirty tricks and even got married to polish her veneer of domestic normalcy. It snowed the judge: despite her well-documented history of instability, she was awarded custody. But she abandoned the act and the showpiece husband as soon as the gavel hit the block.

Like most narcissistic people, my mom was deeply insecure, and she thrived on drama. She couldn't allow her ex to accept the divorce stoically, as he seemed prepared to do. One way or another, she'd make sure he walked away sorry.

So one afternoon she broke into her ex's house. I stayed in the car—which she left running for a quick getaway—wishing for the miraculous power to vanish into thin air and wondering whether it was possible to drop dead from shame. Meanwhile, mom piled every stitch of her ex's clothing on his lawn, doused it with lighter fluid, lit a cigarette, stepped back, and tossed the match onto the heap.

She laughed hysterically the whole way home. She laughed so hard, she cried.

A few months later, Mom burglarized her sister's house, stealing money, guns, jewelry — anything that could be pawned. My family immediately figured out she was the burglar but did nothing. They had given up trying to reform her long ago.

Later, my aunt confronted Mom about it over Thanksgiving dinner. Mom laughingly admitted the caper in an "Aw, shucks" manner. After all, it was a lovable-scamp kind of thing to do, right?

Sadly, that holiday dinner was by no means exceptional. When my family gathered, fireworks followed — drunken fistfights, soap-opera-style accusations, attempted adulterous seductions — the list goes on.

By the time I was thirteen, Mom had shacked up with Lamont. Built like a pygmy gorilla, he had rotting teeth and breath like a geriatric dog's. The should-be-whites of his eyes were yellow like the stains on a chain-smoker's fingers.

His preferred drink was Mickeys — a "fine malt liquor" packaged in green, rounded bottles resembling hand grenades. This was apt, because after he had had a few, his temper was emphatically explosive. He'd down a six-pack over a single commercial break, then beat my mother bloody before the credits rolled. A couple of times, he gave her what he called "flying lessons" by pitching her off our second-story balcony.

But Mom was no Miss Celie—she usually provoked these fights by nagging and needling Lamont until he blew his top and socked her. Then they'd go after one another like wild dogs till dawn.

Meanwhile, I was busy picking up the pieces and hiding our secrets from outsiders because I was terrified of what mom might do if I didn't. I paid bills, forging my mom's signature on checks. I went friendless because I never wanted to have to explain why we couldn't hang out at my house. I learned to cook so I wouldn't go hungry when Mom was too stoned to make dinner. I cleaned vomit off toilets. I vacuumed up broken beer bottles. I learned how to remove blood stains from all kinds of fabric.

And I prayed—day and night—for an escape. But things kept getting worse. I began to suspect that, like my biological father, my heavenly father was too busy or too little interested to listen.

I discovered my mother's crack addiction in the winter of my fourteenth year.

She had all but stopped buying groceries, and our electricity was shut off repeatedly. My half brother Mike showed me how to shoplift in a nearby convenience store. After that, we lived on Frito-Lay and Hostess products. He also showed me how to flip on the electricity after it had been disconnected. So we neither starved nor froze.

But that didn't mean we were safe.

Family meals were always uncomfortable, but the tension skyrocketed when Lamont started showing up fully armed.

One night, we were eating in front of the TV. Lamont mopped up his plate, licked his fingers, and began to polish his gun with the hem of his tattered wife-beater.

He reminded Mike of his impending eighteenth birthday. Then, caressing his gun, he said, "Keep countin' down them days, boy, 'cause you in for a real special birthday surprise."

Lamont got up, slid the revolver into his waistband, and strutted away singing the theme from his favorite show: "Bad boys, bad boys, whatcha gonna do, whatcha gonna do when they come for you?"

One night Mom and Lamont didn't come home, and Mike and I went through their stuff. We found their crack pipe haphazardly hidden under a threadbare nightie. We also found a stack of social security cards about two inches thick.

We figured that was sufficiently incriminating to put them behind bars long enough for us to escape, so we decided to turn them in.

The night of the bust, a SWAT team stormed our apartment, and, for a few moments, Mike and I were facedown on the squalid carpet with guns in our backs. After the SWAT team moved past, a mild-mannered detective shepherded us to his car. In disbelief, we watched as my mother and Lamont, spitting and squirming, were handcuffed and stuffed into a squad car.

Shell-shocked, I looked over at Mike. He appeared giddy as he sang, "Whatcha gonna do when they come for you?"

By this time, I had decided that God was either a myth or a jerk. He never answered my prayers, so either nobody was listening or God had no compassion for the suffering of children. Either way, there was no point in continuing to pray: if the former were true, I'd be talking to myself; if the latter, I didn't want anything to do with such a heartless deity.

Once I was out of imminent danger, I went wild. All the rage and sorrow that had been accumulating over my childhood suddenly burst forth. The flood was so fierce, it threatened to sweep away everything in its path. Like my mother before me, I milked people around me for whatever I could get.

Smoking, vandalism, going to school high, skipping school entirely—you name the delinquent behavior, chances are I did it. I squandered my virginity at fifteen, and by my sixteenth birthday, the number of partners I had had was into double digits. Most were older men I seduced for the things they would give me.

Then I found out I was pregnant. I knew it the moment it happened, as if someone had turned on a light. I knew it, but I didn't want to believe it.

Hoping my gut instinct was faulty, I went to Planned Parenthood for a pregnancy test. It was positive. The counseling I received was not.

The nurse insisted that I must "beg, borrow, and steal" the funds required for an abortion. She even told me how to circumvent my state's parental notification laws, directing me to a no-questions-asked clinic in a bordering state.

I felt I had no choice.

Kurt, my boyfriend, concurred. He came up with his half of the money, and pushed me so forcefully and frequently to follow through that we wound up jumping the gun: when we arrived at the clinic, I wasn't far enough along. We had to return in another few weeks.

Those weeks were a heartache. I'd lie awake into the wee hours trying to convince my child and myself that I wasn't making a terrible mistake. My main rationalization was my fear of doing to my child what my mother had done to me. I'd tell my baby—a girl, I'm certain—"Please, just know that I love you, and that I wish I could've someday held you, but this must be the right thing."

At twenty, I got pregnant a second time—by this time, Kurt and I were married.

I was using a potpourri of recreational drugs and was completely out of touch with my body. By the time I discovered my pregnancy, I had ingested countless drugs known to cause birth defects, which might've severely harmed my child. I was terrified by the thought of carrying to term. And Kurt—still dead set on remaining childless—again vehemently pressured me. Once more, I felt I had no choice.

The second abortion was especially horrific. Pictures of babies the doctor had delivered were *everywhere*—even on the ceiling. Looking down on me were grinning reminders of everything I was throwing away—but it was too late to change my mind. And the physical pain was excruciating. It's quite possible that I left with permanent physical injuries in addition to emotional ones.

Life with Kurt was, in many ways, a grim pantomime of my early family life. We didn't have fistfights like my mother and her men, but we had plenty of nasty arguments. Like my mother, I was profoundly unhappy and used drugs to kill the pain. Kurt, with his countless infidelities and workaholism, left me feeling just as unloved and ignored as had my father.

But something new had been added: Kurt had twice shunned the most fundamental and natural thing I could offer — a child. In so doing, he had abnegated his role as a father, reprising my own broken paternal relationship and the rejection and neglect that I had suffered my entire life.

After five years of marriage, I asked Kurt for a divorce.

I moved to San Francisco. Anonymous there, and unencumbered by my past, I made a fresh start. I found I had many marketable skills and began to freelance in multiple occupations. I also enrolled in a community college.

Meanwhile, I had been experiencing increasingly intense fatigue and pain. I had initially dismissed it, thinking everyone was in agony at the end of the workday. By the time I got my diagnosis — I have a genetic disorder called Ehlers-Danlos syndrome and systemic arthritis caused by an autoimmune disease — I was attending Mills College on a scholarship. Paying my bills while keeping up my high academic standards *and* being sick was practically impossible. I hit a wall.

Facing the end of the month without the next month's rent in hand, I needed to make a lot of money, *fast*. Desperately, I scoured classifieds for a dream-come-true scheme, something that would allow me to work from home. Heck, preferably from bed. But it had to *pay*.

Ads of one sort fit the bill. They appeared in the seedy section of the free papers. They weren't help-wanted ads; they were more like for-sale ads, placed by women with names like Kitty Lovegood and Klassy Sass.

How desperate do you have to be to sink *that* low?

I, for one, was that desperate.

I decided to investigate further.

A web search revealed that those women comprised the market's low-end supply. I could fish farther upstream. I saw that the low-end ladies charged about $200 per hour; if I charged just 50 percent more, I could pay all my bills in no time, leaving me free to focus on school.

It seemed stupid not to try it, but I wanted a controlled environment.

I found a website where call girls networked and advertised, clients commiserated, and girls' services were rated and reviewed. Via that site, I contacted a highly respected madam. She agreed to help me "dip my toe in the water," no strings attached. She'd provide a safe, private location and a client she knew well for my test run. Furthermore, she arranged for me to meet both of them before I decided to go through with anything.

I did exactly that. We three met at the apartment where the madam met her clients. She, the client, and the apartment were all clean, unintimidating, and seemingly normal. I felt at ease.

And the pay was a powerful deal sweetener. I decided to take the plunge.

Initially, I was shy and awkward — then I began to channel my fifteen-year-old self. After that, it was all downhill. Two hours later, the client handed me a white envelope containing several hundred dollars, and I went home and paid my rent.

Then I was off to the races. I adopted a fake name for work, got a second phone for business, and put up an ad. I was officially a working girl.

You can't imagine how often a new girl's phone rings. I'd turn it off for class in the morning, and by midafternoon, my voice mail would be full. It felt exhilarating to be wanted that much, at those prices, by that many men. I was 100 percent dazzled by the whole experience. I had a new spring in my step, a new confidence in my carriage, a whole new self-image.

One who has been rejected or ignored by both parents usually feels defective in some way. One feels unworthy of — or at least not readily capable of enkindling — others' affections.

But in this world, I was the belle of the ball, and being the recipient of such profuse expressions of adoration — mainly from older, middle- to upper-class men with a striking sociocultural similarity to my father — was a wholly new, utterly inebriating experience. Apart from the sexual component, my clients' attentions were facsimiles of the approval I had spent my childhood trying, and failing, to elicit from my father; it felt fantastic finally to receive even this warped version of it.

My reviews were excellent. It seemed I was something rarely seen in that world — a completely unphony girl. Within mere months, I became the Bay Area's top-rated escort.

But something was lacking.

I had no idea what it was, so I tried to fill the void with everything imaginable — booze, drugs, education, hobbies and side jobs, volunteering—you name it. I test-drove virtually every non-Christian belief system but found them all wanting. I couldn't pinpoint their shared shortcoming; I just knew something was missing.

When I hit the top of the escort rankings, I raised my rates and began spending money in an attempt to fill my internal void with possessions. If I wanted something, I bought it.

And I paid cash ... at first. But there were always more things to buy, so I started using credit cards because, hey, the economy was red hot, I was Number One, and my body was a slot machine that kept paying off.

I'd make the money. Tomorrow, if not today. Or maybe next week.

After five years of next weeks, I was drowning in clothes I had never worn, books I hadn't read, movies I couldn't recall, and countless knickknacks. Still, I wasn't satisfied.

And I was getting burned out. I had to have a couple of glasses of wine to put on my service-with-a-smile show.

I needed a change, so I took some massage classes and reinvented myself as a full-body sensual masseuse, or FBSM, provider. This way, I no longer had to offer the whole enchilada, just the rice and beans.

Meanwhile, my debts mounted, and the economy made a U-turn from red hot to ice cold. Luxury services such as FBSM are the first budget item to get axed in lean times. My fiscal flood dwindled to a trickle.

And then, into this disaster walked my next great love. He sat down beside me in a café, told me a very bad joke in a very cute manner, and instantly charmed me.

His name was Tim. He had had a fascinating, adventurous life, and we shared many passions. Most important, he was exceptionally funny in a deadpan, Bill Murrayesque manner.

We began seeing each other often. After a few weeks, I was head over heels. I couldn't bear the guilt of lying to him about my job, so I revealed — and attempted to explain — everything.

He said he couldn't date a sex worker, but I couldn't bear to lose him, so I agreed to quit and give a new job the old college try.

A temp agency placed me as an executive assistant at a utility company. But the executive I was to assist was certifiably nuts, and I had an irresistible impulse to imply as much in every irksome, incomprehensible interaction.

I was fired.

That experience dashed my hopes that I would be able to make a seamless reentry into the average Jane's workforce.

I still had bills to pay, so I began to make surreptitious appointments with old regulars. I kept up the ruse for a few months before Tim caught me red-handed and dumped me.

My debt had spiraled out of control. Bill collectors hounded me relentlessly. I had an occupational albatross around my neck. Add to that the loss of the one bright spot in my life, and you have a recipe for disaster.

I was on numerous heavy-duty prescription medications and had just had them refilled. I had a month's supply of everything.

I lined up the bottles up in a neat row, like soldiers marching in to obliterate the enemy.

I was that enemy.

I choked down more than five hundred pills, including enough morphine to fell a gorilla. Then I put on a favorite movie and settled down to sleep forever.

It was three days before I was found.

Earlier, I had made a lunch date with a fellow who had transitioned from client to friend, and when he arrived to pick me up, he could tell something was very wrong. He called my best friend, Juliette, who came over immediately.

By the time she got me to the ER, it was far too late to pump my stomach. The hospital staff was astounded by my survival; some referred to it as "miraculous."

While I was in the hospital, Juliette collected funds from my friends and got my bills current. She took care of all my life's tedious details, leaving me free to focus on getting well. She devised a plan for my transition back into a world without sex work, including a budget and a free room in her home until I got on my feet.

She, in cooperation with the grace of God, saved my life.

Although I was still pro-choice, I had been steadily growing more conservative, politically and morally speaking, since about midway through my years as an escort. One day after I had successfully escaped sex work and built a new foundation for my life, I was listening to Mike Huckabee's radio show while driving over the Bay Bridge. He spoke about a woman in the news who was arrested for drowning her baby in a toilet after giving birth in a pub bathroom. Huckabee remarked that if she had gone to Planned Parenthood a few weeks earlier, she would've gotten off scot-free. Instead, she was facing a first-degree murder charge.

I had to admit he had a point; it didn't make sense for her to be innocent one week and a murderess the next for doing essentially the same thing. And if the dividing line between murder and the elimination of unwanted tissue wasn't within the last few weeks of gestation, when was it? I had studied enough biology to know there's no magic moment in which a preborn human suddenly metamorphoses from a blob to a baby. That was a fairy tale told to placate women like me, who had murdered their children, or who were contemplating doing so.

I couldn't defeat the logic of his argument, so I became pro-life then and there.

That marked the removal of the last ideological difference between the Church's teachings and my opinions, although I didn't realize it at the time. Within days, I started noticing bumper stickers for Catholic radio. The first time I saw one, I thought, "What on earth could they possibly find to talk about twenty-four hours a day?" The concept seemed slightly absurd to me.

But I kept seeing the stickers. Eventually, my curiosity got the better of me, and I began to tune in. What I heard them saying was so intriguing that I woke up one Sunday morning with a clear purpose: *I'm gonna give this Catholic thing a go.* My need to get to Mass that day became as urgent as my need to breathe.

I didn't know any Catholics and was completely ignorant about Church practices, so, in search of a homey-feeling parish, I bumbled about in trial-and-error fashion until I stumbled into a Traditional Latin Mass. I knew the moment I walked in that I had hit the jackpot. There I found all the majesty that an institution founded by Jesus Himself ought rightly to possess.

I left in tears, born not of sorrow, but, rather, of sheer joy and the shock of the sublime.

All humans want and need a family. I never really had a proper one — indeed, I've often joked that I was raised by wolves. But underneath the levity, my craving for the kind of intimate community that's supposed to exist within families runs deep, and the pain caused by the lack thereof has been visceral and unremitting. Indeed, there has been a yawning chasm in my life where a cohesive and caring family should be.

For my part, I squandered my God-given opportunities to build my own family. Paralyzed by fears arising from the dysfunctional circumstances in which I grew up, and by my desire to avoid repeating my parents' mistakes, I committed far graver crimes. Although my parents — often unwittingly — rejected and neglected me through thoughtless words and cold silence, unkind deeds and indifferent inaction, I rejected my own children in a far more overt and irreversible way. Robbing someone of his life and disposing of him like so much rubbish is the cruelest rejection possible. In the end, all I got for it was another gaping void: every day, I'm painfully aware of the two empty places in my life where my children ought to be.

Ultimately, the key reasons I became, and remain, Catholic relate to the Church's teachings on life and the source from which new life springs — the family.

First, Church doctrine concerning the family's proper province and practices rang true and jibed with my experiences. I know too well that functional families are essential foundations for fostering future fruition. Not having had one, I've had to struggle far harder than my peers just to get my head above water.

Second, Catholicism's function as an ancient, universal spiritual family in which all are welcome and everyone has a meaningful role afforded me an opportunity to revise my life's narrative in a profound way. Here was a community in which I finally found the unconditional love I had desperately and vainly sought from my parents. In stark contrast to my childhood role as catastrophe-camouflage coordinator, in the Church family I could productively participate in countless joyful, healthy ways.

Third, I was galvanized by the fact that a family—one not merely functional, but *holy*—lay at the core of Catholic theology. Within that family are parents anyone would be proud to call his own. First Mary, literally the perfect mother: she was created free from the stain of original sin and resisted innumerable temptations and distractions from the fallen world around her, placing her familial role above all else. Then Joseph, imperfect like the rest of us, but possessed of the exceptional faithfulness, obedience, and divine trust that allows fallen creatures to soar in virtue. Mary and Jospeh were worth emulating, and available as surrogate parents for those in need—folks like me.

Finally, the Church was the only place where I heard the whole truth about my abortions. Everyone else tried to placate me into believing I had made a "hard choice," but ultimately had done the "right thing." My heart knew that was a lie. I was sick of being lied to, and sick to the depths of my soul on account of what I had done. The Church offered me remedies for both ailments.

The priest who catechized me confirmed that I had committed a grave sin; at the same time, he laid out a clear path to reconciliation with God, and affirmed the tiny shred of hope I had been hesitantly cultivating all those years: the hope that my children were somewhere I might be able to go to in the life to come; the hope that someday I might finally lay eyes upon them;

and the hope that the oppressive emptiness left in the wake of their violent deaths might be filled.

You cannot imagine how valuable that hope is to me — how much it helps me get through tough times.

I came to my first Mass with jumbled expectations. I hoped at least to find like-minded people with whom I might socialize. But I found so much more. I found the family I never had; the love I had been forever seeking; the truth for which I had been thirsting; and a place to heal old wounds.

In short, I found a place in which I can truly live.

At long last, I found my home.

ANNEMARIE SCHREIBER is a writer, seamstress, and nanny. She's crazy about history and historical artifacts, including classic films and anything vintage. Volunteer work, particularly for the Church, is her driving passion. She lives and works in the San Francisco Bay area and feels very blessed to do so.

ANNEMARIESCHREIBER77@GMAIL.COM

ABORTION TO ADORATION

JEWELS GREEN

I heard the nurse before I saw her.

"Hello, honey. It's time to wake up. You're in the recovery room."

The pain in my abdomen was supposed to be a welcome sign that the abortion was a success, that my crisis was over. My burden had been lifted, or forcibly removed, and I was supposed to be grateful, relieved, prepared to move on.

Instead, I already felt myself slipping.

Unsteady on my feet, aching in my belly, I stumbled out of the recovery room.

Outside, snow on the ground made walking even more difficult. There were no people with signs, like the ones you always see on the news. Nobody had been there two days earlier, either, when I couldn't go through with it, when I ran out to an empty parking lot, trying to save my baby.

And nobody was there on my way in this morning.

Nobody.

> *I wanted my baby.*
> *My baby was dead.*
> *I wanted to join him.*

Hours passed. I was seventeen, a high school dropout working midnight shift at a convenience store. And I hated myself.

How had I let this happen? When I found out I was pregnant, I had decided to keep my baby. I stopped using drugs. I went to the library and checked out a book called *Under 18 and Pregnant.* One of the chapters described the comfort of maternity undies. I wanted some. I called the welfare office to get on medical assistance. I made a prenatal-care appointment.

But nobody wanted my baby but me.

And I was not enough.

For years, I had believed in a "woman's right to choose"; and I expected that after the abortion, my life would change for the better. Instead, where I had once been full and warm, I was now cold, empty, and raw. I missed my baby. I mourned him. It was my fault he was dead. I was guilty and would never forgive myself.

About six weeks after my abortion, I decided I was no longer worthy of life. I determined to end it. It was time to go.

Years before, I had discovered that cutting myself helped me cope with emotional pain. It was abnormal and wrong, but it was effective.

I was a quick cutter.

Slice, slice, slice.

Each cut brought me closer to calm: transforming my inner pain into physical pain mitigated it. My body took control of my mind. The bloodletting ritual left me stoically in control. Afterward, during the methodical cleaning and dressing of my wounds and the blade, I grew serene. Later, the ache under the bandages reminded that I had the power to banish my errant emotions.

I didn't want to die; I just preferred physical pain to emotional pain, and most certainly it was better than numbness. When I had cut myself in the past, I hadn't wanted to die.

This time was different.

I had read that blood flowed more freely under warm water, so I started filling the tub. I knelt next to it, lowered my arms into the water, and slashed both forearms. I waited, but didn't die.

It was taking too long, so I shook the water off my bloody arms, opened the medicine cabinet, found some prescription pills, and took them all. Still no death.

I turned on the oven.

I knelt on the cold, cracked linoleum floor of my cheap basement apartment and stuck my head in.

Although I grew up loving God and going to Sunday School every week at a Lutheran church where I loved the pastor, I hadn't prayed or been to church in over a year. Now I prayed . . . for death.

When the paramedics pounded on the door, I wouldn't let them in. At some point I must have called my boyfriend, and he must have called 911. I don't know how the paramedics got into the apartment, but when they saw me, they laughed. They laughed at my cuts, at the empty pill bottle, at the hot kitchen with the oven door open. They laughed at the teenager with eyebrows and bangs singed because she hadn't blown out the pilot light.

"Guess you didn't really want to die, huh?"

I wanted my baby.

My baby was dead.

But I was not.

I was devastated, a failure.

I couldn't even kill myself. Worse, I was now a burden to my mother, to the hospital staff, and even to the health-care system. (I really thought about this. I mean, weren't there people who were *really* sick who needed my hospital bed?)

I spent my first night in a solitary observation room in the adolescent psychiatric unit, within sight of the nurses' station. At first I was belligerent, but soon found comforting the presence of other teens in pain. I was no longer alone. I adjusted to the psych-unit routine, participated in individual and group therapy, and got stabilized on psych medication. That month in the hospital saved my life. My abortion still haunted me — especially at night — but it no longer monopolized my every waking thought.

I wanted my baby.

My baby was dead.

I tried to justify it.

On April 9, 1989, just a few weeks after I was discharged from the hospital, I rode a packed bus to Washington, DC, to participate in the "March for Women's Lives" with thousands of other abortion rights activists. I carried a sign featuring a coat hanger inside a red circle with a slash through it. A few weeks later, I began volunteering as a patient escort at a first-trimester abortion facility.

You'd think that my abortion and suicide attempt would have made me pro-life. The opposite happened. My pro-abortion convictions hardened. I ceased being merely a believer in "a woman's right to choose" and became an activist.

After a few months as a volunteer escort, I was hired at an abortion clinic full-time—just one year after my abortion and less than a year after my suicide attempt.

Now I see that I was trying to obliterate my guilt; then it did not seem incongruous for me to spend my days defending unfettered "reproductive rights" and my nights sobbing about my lost baby.

I knew my original due date and often thought about how old my child would have been on any given day. The anniversary of my abortion and the anniversary of my due date were always hard. I missed my baby and knew that I would never—ever—have another abortion, yet I still thought it was acceptable for other women to exercise their "right to choose" at the hands of my coworkers.

Years later I learned in graduate school that holding such incompatible views is called cognitive dissonance, and it creates stress. There are many ways to cope with the stress, some healthy (such as changing behavior or attitudes to be consistent with beliefs and actions) and some not (such as avoiding the conflict, hiding from it, pretending it doesn't exist, or trying to justify it).

My deep, hidden, overwhelming need to disabuse myself of blame meant that I was always projecting my vulnerable, fragile, younger self onto the weepier patients. I would coo, "It's going to be all right."

I surrounded myself with people who thought abortion was okay, even often laudable, hoping that someday I would believe that, too, and could stop torturing myself. I desperately wanted someone to assure me that it was going to be all right.

On and off, I worked at the clinic for five years. Strangely, some of my fondest memories are from my time there. Most of my coworkers were smart, independent, dedicated, and trustworthy women. I admired them and was inspired by them. We all genuinely believed that we were providing a necessary, innocuous medical service to women who would otherwise take matters into their own hands and bleed to death in seedy hotel rooms. This created a camaraderie I've not experienced in any other workplace.

But there were also times when using distraction to hold my cognitive dissonance at bay failed. When I was hired, I answered phones and booked appointments. Every few months I learned a new job: front-desk receptionist, payment collection, medical assisting (pregnancy test and vital signs), pre-abortion and recovery-room counseling, after-hours emergency medical response, and autoclave technician. The joke was that I was the "poster child for cross-training" because I did every job there except doctor and nurse. I even came in early to sweep up cigarette butts outside and spent one of my Sundays painting the staff bathroom after the clinic was remodeled.

Occasionally, when I worked as a counselor, a woman asked me to accompany her into the procedure room to hold her hand during the abortion. Of course, this was only if she was going to be awake with local anesthetic. If she was to receive intravenous sedation, she would be asleep and wouldn't know what was going on or if anyone was holding her hand or not. I had been asleep for my abortion.

I was in the procedure room as a hand holder probably a dozen times, but one time hit close to home.

It was the first time.

The patient was almost ten weeks pregnant and nineteen years old, the same age I was. And I had also been almost ten weeks pregnant when I had my abortion.

Her grip was tight.

"Everything's going to be all right," I lied. She looked at me for a moment and probably didn't believe me, then squeezed her eyes shut. Her breath caught and she silently started to cry.

"There's still time to change your mind," the doctor said. "Are you sure this is what you want to do?"

She nodded and squeaked out a small yes.

The sound of the machine was always the worst part.

When the hard-plastic hollow tube forced into a woman's uterus hit something more solid and liquid, the sound of suctioning abruptly changed. Imagine enjoying a homemade strawberry milkshake with a straw—then you hit a piece of strawberry. There is a sudden stop, followed by a rapid decrease in pitch and timbre of the sucking sound.

It's heartbreaking. I will never forget that sound.

At the clinic, I sometimes worked as the dishwasher. I scrubbed used, bloodied tools until they were shiny again, put them into a metal tray, wrapped it all up with blue paper like a present, and then popped the whole kit into an autoclave, a machine like a microwave that is used to sterilize metal surgical instruments.

The autoclave room looked like a galley kitchen. There were two sinks, one on the left counter and one on the right counter. Above each of the countertops was a little door that concealed a small hole in the wall, a window into each of the two procedure rooms. After an abortion, the instrument tray was passed through the window in the wall into the autoclave room. The other thing that passed through was the Jar. It held the precious contents that just moments before had comfortably resided inside the mother's womb.

It looked like an oversized glass pickle jar. It was emptied next to me on to the countertop: teeny-tiny hands and feet and arms and legs and a rib cage and a spine and a hollow, flattened, misshapen, torn head.

I saw it all.

I smelled it all.

Every time. Up to thirty times a day, four days a week.

Before then, I had had dreams about my abortion, about my baby, and how different my life would've been had I let him live.

Now I started having nightmares, haunted by tiny, limbless phantom babies. I was floating down a narrow stream with miniature body parts strewn on either shore — and then I'd begin to sink. I'd flail and gasp and go under.

I was twenty years old when I told the clinic director, "I'm having nightmares. Does anyone else have nightmares when working autoclave?"

She replied, "What we do here is end a life. It's that simple. It's basic. And if you're not okay with that, you can't work here."

My schedule was changed for the next few weeks to give me a rest from the autoclave room. I took patients' vital signs in the recovery room, counseled women before their abortions, and ran pregnancy tests in the lab. The next time I met with the clinic director, I assured her that I was on board with the work we did, and with our mission and dedication to preserving women's reproductive rights.

At the time, this was more than just lip service. I told myself that abortion was alright for *other* women, even though it had been dead wrong for me. I loved my job at the clinic, even though it gave me nightmares. While most of my friends were working at drugstores, retail shops, or work-study during college, I had a job with a purpose, and they envied me. I tried to keep my pesky conscience muzzled.

═══°σ°═══

There were times when anti-abortion forces made this easier.

On the morning of Wednesday, July 17, 1991, a woman buzzed the intercom and asked to come in for a pregnancy test. When she opened the door, she and her compatriots ran into the waiting room, plopped down a 200-pound metal contraption with pipes sticking out at different angles, and started throwing chairs. Then they all got on the floor and somehow attached themselves to the metal device by placing their arms down the pipes.

I was terrified.

Someone smarter than I am quickly guessed that it probably wasn't a bomb or the people who carried it into the waiting room wouldn't have attached themselves to it. We herded frightened patients and their drivers down the hallway that led to the medical area of the clinic, behind a locked steel door with bulletproof glass. They sat in the staff lunchroom, which became our makeshift waiting room, while we called the police.

The invading protesters spent seven hours on the waiting-room floor while police negotiated with them and made multiple attempts to free them from the device. They sang, they chanted, and they would not leave.

We met patients outside, explained what was going on, and led them up a back stairway directly to the staff lunchroom in the secure medical area. I recall that more than a dozen abortions were performed while the trespassers were in the waiting room.

The immediate effects of the invasion were the opposite of their intent. Patients and those accompanying them seemed to steel their resolve in the face of the threat. I don't recall anyone being ambivalent that day. Many patients were angry. We staff members were galvanized into action as "comrades in arms" as we went about our duties, determined not to let law-breaking extremists stop us. At the end of the day, after all the patients left and the protesters were removed, we celebrated.

If the autoclave nightmares had begun to awaken moral misgivings about my job, they were banished not only by the invasion, but by far worse events.

On March 10, 1993, Dr. David Gunn got out of his car in the parking lot of his Pensacola, Florida, abortion clinic. A man shouted, "Don't kill any more babies!" and shot him in the back three times. Dr. Gunn left behind a wife and two children, one

of whom I later met and joined in lobbying the federal govern-
ment to use antiracketeering laws against violent anti-abortion
protesters.

There were other well-known murders of doctors and staff
who worked at abortion facilities. I signed sympathy cards that
were sent to the families of Dr. John Britton and James Barrett
just a little over a year after Dr. Gunn was shot. Then, on December 30, 1994, two women were killed at a clinic shooting
in Boston.

I imagine that some people left their jobs at abortion clinics
after that. I didn't quit, but I did wear a bulletproof vest to work
for a full week after the Boston killings. During this scary time, I
had more nightmares about being killed at work than I did about
the killing going on in the procedure rooms.

These terrible events solidified my pro-choice ideology into
a steadfast commitment to ensuring that abortion would remain
a legal option for pregnant women.

> *I wanted my baby.*
> *My baby was dead.*
> *I tried to ignore it.*

I wish I could say that I left my job at the clinic because I had an
intense conversion that left me unable to stomach the whole-
sale slaughter of babies, but that's not what happened. I left
to go to graduate school in New York City. Even though I no
longer worked in a clinic or considered myself an activist, I was
staunchly pro-choice and even more staunchly an atheist.

Enrolled full-time in a doctoral program in health psychology,
I focused my energy on neuropsychology, working three part-time

jobs to house and feed myself. I was one of the few non-Jews in a Jewish university, where my professors and classmates openly and often talked about their faith. There I first met Orthodox Jews. I found it fascinating that they loved their God and their faith so much that it became for them a complete way of life, determining the way they dressed, what they ate, when their children got their first haircut, what language they prayed in, and so much more. Now I believe that my interest betrayed a deeper, hidden desire to know God.

I left grad school early with a master of arts degree, landing a job at the prestigious Memorial Sloan Kettering Cancer Center in Manhattan working as a research assistant in the Department of Surgery. I encountered far more death at this job than at the abortion facility, but this place was also filled with hope, promise, and occasional joy. There had been no joy at the abortion clinic.

During my three years working at Sloan Kettering I experienced tremendous growth and change. My husband and I met and married during my time there, and it's where God found me, or rather, where I finally answered Him.

Along the hallway to the cafeteria at the center was a small interfaith chapel, meant to be a quiet place for patients and their loved ones to reflect and pray. I had seen other employees walk through the chapel door before, but for months I had walked past it, keenly aware of the sacredness of the space beyond that door, and wildly curious behind my stubbornly secular, scientific veneer.

Then one day, I'm not sure why, I stopped in front of the door and opened it. The chapel was small, dimly lit, and felt undeniably sacred. That first time, all I did was peek in before going back to work.

The next day, I went inside and sat down on one of the pews for a few minutes. I don't remember what, if anything, I thought about while I was there, but I remember feeling at peace. Every day after lunch, I sat quietly in the chapel for a few minutes. My belief in God rekindled and then strengthened with each visit, not because of that particular prayer space, but because I allowed myself to search inside of me for prayer space.

It wasn't until a few years later, after leaving New York City and my job at Sloan Kettering, that I began going to church. My husband and I attended the Lutheran church where I grew up, mostly to prepare for the baptism of our first son.

My husband was raised Catholic, his uncle was a priest, and his great-uncle had been a Franciscan brother; but my husband was not practicing his Faith. We weren't even married in a church, but in a hot air balloon in Las Vegas by a minister of the United Church of Christ. My husband agreed to attend Lutheran worship services with me and to have our three sons baptized in the Lutheran church.

During this time, I remained pro-choice, although I did not donate to the cause or attend rallies. I even worked at the abortion facility part-time throughout my pregnancy with our first son. I would waddle across the parking lot wearing surgical scrubs stretched tight against my huge belly and protesters would shout, "Your baby loves you!" I would smile because I loved him, too.

I stopped working at the abortion clinic after my first son was born. Indeed, I stopped working outside the home altogether because I felt called to full-time motherhood. My husband and I sacrificed to make it work. We began attending a Lutheran church more regularly after our second and third sons were born. I volunteered on the preschool committee, and we participated in fellowship events at church, but neither of us ever felt at home there. We talked about this, but never with the goal of finding a solution; and we never discussed the possibility of my becoming Catholic, or of our family trying out another faith.

Everything changed in November of 2010. Still considering myself a pro-choice Lutheran, I was involved in an online group discussion of in vitro fertilization (IVF). I confess that I had never given it much thought, but being a scientifically minded modern woman, I lumped IVF in with other "reproductive rights" that I assumed were essential to maintaining equality for women.

There were about ten women in the discussion group. We had all been chatting with each other for six years, having initially "met" online in a discussion group for natural childbirth. Two of the women were faithful Catholics. I credit these two women with planting the seeds of my eventual conversion — both to the pro-life worldview and to embracing the Catholic Faith — by inviting me to question my deeply held, yet unexamined, opinions.

They were not aggressive or condescending, but both calmly and firmly held their ground, although outnumbered by the opposition, remaining steadfast in their defense of the sanctity and dignity of the lives of the unborn, including microscopic, homeless embryos. Before I encountered their compassionate, unyielding witness, I didn't know what the Catholic Church taught about the sanctity of human life.

I became uncomfortable as I read more about IVF. I didn't know that for every child born as a result of IVF procedures, four or five embryos are created. These "extras" are destroyed or kept frozen until they are discarded or, more rarely, adopted. It was difficult to accept that death was the eventual fate of most of the little cold souls in the IVF clinic freezers around the world.

As I struggled to reconcile my pro-choice convictions with my growing unease with this inhumane practice, one of the members of our discussion group announced that she had agreed to be a gestational surrogate for a couple who were friends of hers. Eventually she became pregnant with this couple's child and shared stories of her experience as a member of a support group for surrogate mothers. She told us that one woman's surrogacy contract included a stipulation for genetic testing on the growing baby. When the results showed the baby would be born with Down syndrome, this surrogate was offered payment of her contract *in full* to abort.

And she did.

That was it. Here, finally, was my aha! moment. This woman was paid to kill the baby she had been contractually obligated to gestate for paying customers. She was paid the full amount of her contract as if she had carried to term and delivered the child.

Most likely it was tens of thousands of dollars. Now pregnancy was a financial transaction, with children as commodities made, bought, sold, and destroyed for quality control. This was fundamentally wrong.

Once I admitted that *this* abortion was wrong, it was not hard to realize that *all* abortion is wrong. To be intellectually honest and consistent, I could no longer remain pro-choice.

I was now pro-life.

Now what?

I couldn't just be pro-life at home. I needed forgiveness. I needed atonement. I needed to *do* something.

I approached my Lutheran pastor to discuss the possibility of arranging a fund-raiser for a local pregnancy resource center. I was unprepared for his strong opposition. He explained that the social statement of the Evangelical Lutheran Church in America (ELCA) was essentially pro-choice. I was shocked. Even if the ELCA was pro-choice, surely our church could see the benefit of helping local mothers with ultrasounds, counseling, baby clothes, parenting classes, and other basic necessities. Nope. My request to collect donations was flatly denied, and I left church that day feeling confused and betrayed.

Then the real soul-searching began.

Was I upset with my pastor, or with my religion? Did I want my children to be raised in a pro-choice religion? I thought of my strong Catholic friends, both online and in my day-to-day life, and I knew they were 100 percent pro-life, but I didn't quite know why. I was attracted to the idea that right and wrong are fixed moral concepts, not bound by individual whims or the social customs of a particular time or era. In the Catholic Church, surprisingly, truth was not decided by popular vote.

I started to research the Catholic Faith in earnest.

I searched online for "pro-life Catholic," and the results included a link to *The Angelica Joy Story*, a documentary about a devout Catholic family blessed with ten children, who learned that the mother's next child in utero had a rare, fatal genetic disorder that routinely caused babies to live for only a few hours after birth. Remaining faithful to the Catholic Church's teaching, her parents refused abortion and instead chose to carry their baby girl to term. She lived for five months and brought immense joy to everyone she met. Her family shared their gratitude for the time they spent with her during her short life.

What struck me, other than the tremendous courage and strength of this remarkable family, was their constant faith in God's plan. Included in the film was a beautiful shot of Angelica's mother staring at what I now know was a monstrance. I did not know what it was at the time, and when I heard her voice-over say, "As I again was graced with the opportunity to spend time in the Adoration chapel," I was mystified.

Adoration chapel? Adoration? What was that?

I remembered hearing that Catholics believe that during the Consecration the Host "becomes" Jesus, but I didn't understand what that meant or why it mattered until I delved deeper into Catholicism.

I especially loved reading conversion stories. I devoured those of Scott and Kimberly Hahn, Heather King, and especially the accounts of former Lutherans compiled in Tim Drake's book *There We Stood, Here We Stand: Eleven Lutherans Rediscover Their Catholic Roots*.

Learning the true meaning of the Real Presence of Jesus in the Eucharist was a turning point for me. I hungered to receive Him in the Blessed Sacrament and be a part of the Body of Christ. I longed for the gift and grace of forgiveness in the sacrament of Reconciliation. I needed to be a part of the Church founded by Jesus, with a direct line of apostolic succession, and where truth was unchanging and eternal.

I wanted to be Catholic.

I called my husband's uncle, a priest and pastor of a parish, and spent more than an hour on the phone, asking him questions.

A dear friend took me to my first Mass, and I was moved to tears. Just outside the entrance of the church was a statue of a weeping angel dedicated to all the children killed by abortion.

I was home.

I picked up a copy of *Catholicism for Dummies* and registered for the Rite of Christian Initiation of Adults (RCIA). Different parishioners taught the classes each week: a few lifelong Catholics, a few converts, one man studying to be a permanent deacon, and the priest.

After a few classes, I felt it was time for me to visit the Perpetual Adoration chapel.

The Adoration chapel in the 130-year-old gray stone church was tiny and was used as the children's chapel during Mass. It had five pews, one loud, hissing, overactive radiator, two beautiful stained-glass windows, and one brilliant monstrance embracing and displaying the consecrated Host. The first time I opened the chapel door I could sense the presence of something unspeakably holy.

I closed the door behind me as gently and silently as I could, dipped my fingers into the wall-mounted font of holy water, blessed myself, turned to face the monstrance, and promptly fell to both knees on the floor. That first time I hadn't even made it as far as a pew, much less a kneeler. I held my head in my hands for a moment, collected myself, and finally rose to sign in as a visitor on the adorer schedule. I slid into the last pew, lowered the kneeler, glanced up at the Blessed Sacrament for a moment, then closed my eyes, and put my head back into my hands, begging for forgiveness.

My reaction upon entering the Adoration Chapel for the first time reminded me of the only other time I spontaneously and involuntarily fell to my knees, overwhelmed with prayers of praise and thanksgiving: when I learned I was expecting my firstborn son. I knew I was finally on the right path.

The RCIA process was exciting, illuminating, and at times daunting. The teachers and priests welcomed my questions and always pointed me to Sacred Scripture and the writings of the early Church Fathers. The beauty of Church teaching on the inherent dignity of every human life combined with the Real Presence of Christ in the Eucharist kept me straight on the path to becoming Catholic. By His grace, I was received into the Catholic Church during the Easter Vigil, 2012.

Although being a faithful Catholic is not easy, it is right, and it is what God wants for me. I am convinced it's what God wants for all of us. I learn more about my Faith every day and am immensely grateful for the sacraments. My first Reconciliation, Confirmation, first Holy Communion, and the convalidation of my marriage are among the true highlights of my life. Our children are being raised in the Catholic Faith; we pray together; we attend the Holy Sacrifice of the Mass together; and we go to Reconciliation together as a family.

We are home.

I wanted my baby.
My baby is dead.
I accept it.

In the Church that Jesus founded there is a place for my suffering. There is a place for my baby's suffering. There is a place for your suffering.

It is the Spirit himself bearing witness with our spirit that we are children of God, and if children, then heirs, heirs of God and fellow heirs with Christ, provided we suffer with him in order that we may also be glorified with him (Romans 8:16–17).

Truth lives in the Catholic Church, and this Truth will set you free.

I want my baby.
My baby is dead.
I tell my story.

JEWELS GREEN is a regretful, repentant post-abortive mother, suicide-attempt survivor, and former abortion clinic worker turned ardent human-rights advocate. She is a writer and a public speaker, has appeared on TV and radio programs, and is featured in the documentary film 40. Jewels lives in the suburbs of Philadelphia, where her full-time job is stay-at-home mother to three wonderful sons.

JEWELS@JEWELSGREEN.COM

WWW.JEWELSGREEN.COM

A TEXAS BAPTIST MEETS THE GOOD SHEPHERD IN ROME

LETICIA OCHOA ADAMS

My grandparents were married in the Catholic Church, but I don't know why: after their last child was baptized, they never went to church. When I was born, my father abandoned my mother, so my grandfather claimed me as his own, and I was given his last name.

My grandfather died when I was three years old.

My mother took his death pretty hard and decided to move to South Texas near my *tio* (uncle) Roy. That's how I ended up in the small town of Three Rivers. Everything about that move changed the course of my life and landed me right where I am now, writing this chapter for you to read.

At my grandfather's funeral, my tio picked me up and carried me to the open coffin so that I could say my final good-bye to the man I had loved like a father for my entire three years of life.

Ten months ago, I carried my own three-year-old granddaughter to the coffin that my tio Roy lay in.

Tio Roy was a constant in my life, a pillar of stability. It wasn't until his coffin was put in the ground that I realized that I do know who I am and where I come from.

We lived in Three Rivers until my mom got a job in Kenedy, a town thirty minutes away. We visited my tio and tia almost every weekend. My tio worked for the local funeral home and was close friends with the man who ran it, Jerry Adams. Jerry had two kids with his wife, Irene. My tia would watch them sometimes, and she would watch me, too.

One day, the little boy, Stacey Adams, talked me into playing in my tia's sewing closet, which was not a good idea. We made a mess! She found us, yelled at us, and gave me a spanking. The face of the little boy Stacey was burned into my memory. I now carry his last name since he is my husband. Funny how life works, right?

Strangers always assumed I was Mexican because we spoke Spanish and worked in the fields. My folks didn't encourage me to learn to read or write and looked down on my attempts to do so. So I spent lots of time alone, estranged from my heritage and my family.

A BAPTIST MEETS THE GOOD SHEPHERD

I didn't speak English when I started school. The school told my mom that I needed to learn English or I was going to be put in special-ed classes. That was it! I was no longer allowed to speak Spanish at home. Everyone around me stopped talking to me in the only language I had ever known and started talking to me only in English. I had no idea why or what I had done for everyone to stop talking to me in a way I could understand.

We moved into a house with a man named Manuel. He lived in the back room, so we shared only the kitchen. My mom and I shared the front bedroom, and the living room was ours. There was a huge yard plus three acres in the back that I could run around in. It was where I spent most of my time; just me, my thoughts, my journals, my books, and music. I had a tree house that was really just an old painter's scaffold in between two trees, but it was all I needed. I was an only child, so being alone with my thoughts and books was normal for me.

I was just a little girl with no real sense of the fact that I didn't have a father or that my mother lived with a man who molested me as my mother cleaned the kitchen and as he taught me English (don't ask me, it's just how it went down); or that my life would be full of heartbreak, tears, and drama.

Manuel was a mechanic with a garage next to our house. He was one of the few father figures in my life from the age of five until I ran away for the last time when I was fifteen. I have a lot of great memories of him in my life, but I also know exactly what he did to me for years when he sexually abused me. Every doubt I ever had that I was wrong about it vanished on the day I stood on his front porch a year ago and told him to his face that I remembered it all, followed by the words "I forgive you."

I didn't do it because I'm such a great Catholic; I did it because after years of therapy, I realized I needed to see his face when I told him that I knew he had molested and raped me for years before I turned nine years old. I needed to be free and the only way to get that freedom was to forgive him. God can punish him; that's not my job.

After I forgave Manuel, my husband, Stacey, and I walked through the field where I had spent so much time daydreaming as a child. The spring wildflowers were blooming as if to welcome me home and remind me of all the great things in my childhood that I was now free to remember, since what that man did to me no longer ruled my memory.

When I was eight years old, one of the families that my mom babysat for invited me to the local First Baptist Church for vacation Bible school. I had so much fun there that I began to attend this church regularly. I would walk there every chance I got. I went all by myself to Sunday school and services plus any other day there was something going on.

By the time I was twelve, I had answered so many altar calls that I lost count. Each time, I would kneel at the altar and pray the sinner's prayer, hoping that this was the time when Jesus would become real to me. I looked around me and saw that He was real to all the other kids in my middle school youth group, but for me, Jesus was just an idea. I knew of Him and what He did for me; I knew the Bible; but I didn't personally know Jesus Himself.

If you had asked me, though, I would've said that I had a personal relationship with Him! I had no idea what that actually meant, and nobody would really answer that for me, but I assumed I did because I was doing all the Christian things.

Like most teen girls my age in the sixth grade, I loved New Kids on the Block. I would daydream about Donnie Wahlberg coming into town and falling in love with me. We would ride away together to get married and live happily ever after. My wall was plastered with giant posters of him. I was obsessed to the max.

One day after history class, I was standing next to my locker, talking to my best friend, when this boy walked down the hallway: Stacey Adams, whom I had played with as a child. He had on a white T-shirt, its sleeves rolled up, jeans, and white high-tops. He walked like a bad boy and looked just like Donnie Wahlberg.

I fell in love with him at that very moment. I don't remember the details, but I stalked him until he finally kissed me on the steps of the First Baptist Church, where I learned about Jesus.

After that kiss, Jesus was no longer the reason I went to church every chance I got. Stacey was: my first love. I loved everything about him and forgot about having a personal relationship with Jesus.

I was almost fourteen by the time the issue of sex came up. I knew that sex outside of marriage was a sin, and I didn't want to do anything that would make me not be a Christian, but I really loved Stacey, and it just seemed like the thing to do. All the girls my age were having sex with their boyfriends.

I didn't just want to sleep with him though; I wanted a life with him. We made plans for the big moment, but I did the one thing that's better than any kind of birth control: I told Stacey that I loved him and wanted to have his babies.

That, combined with the fact that I suddenly realized what sex was, and that I had already done this before but with Manuel when I was a little girl, caused the entire thing to fall apart.

We didn't go through with it, and we broke up. He ended up going out with and sleeping with one of my close friends. The heartbreak and betrayal plus the awakened memories of my sexual abuse created a perfect storm.

I assumed that God hated me or didn't care about me because all the other people I saw having a relationship with Jesus were getting everything they wanted. They had families, dads, and boyfriends. They were pretty and popular. I had none of those things, and I was the girl with the reputation, once I started sleeping around, which I did out of a sense of taking back control over what happened to my body. I decided that being good had done nothing for me: I would go my way, and God could go His.

Within a year, I had slept with more guys than most women sleep with in their entire lives. Only recently did I realize that I never enjoyed any of it. I just wanted to be loved, to have someone claim me as his own, and to soothe the pain I was in. None of that happened. With each guy, I just added to the pain.

I believed I was bad and unwanted. That made me an easy target for guys wanting to take advantage of me. And there were plenty of guys happy to do just that. It was as if I had a sign on my forehead.

At sixteen, I wasn't going to the mall or to concerts with friends; I was working full-time, going to school, and pregnant. I had taken my first pregnancy test in the bathroom of the Long John Silver's, where I worked. I stared at the two pink lines, not knowing if I should be scared or if this was the answer to all my prayers.

I wasn't sure how was going to tell my mom, but I didn't think that telling the father would be an issue. I figured he would be freaked out but he would marry me and we would be a family. His father was a deacon in the Catholic Church, so I was sure that his family would encourage him to marry me.

I was wrong.

I mean, they might have tried to tell him to marry me, but I didn't know that, and he sure didn't listen if they did.

His first suggestion was for me to have an abortion. I would like to say that I knew that I was carrying a life and that abortion would end that life, but really it was pure stubbornness that made me tell him where he could shove that suggestion: I didn't need his help.

I was right.

I didn't. That child is now twenty-two years old, and I have asked his father's help only once in all those years.

When I was nineteen, I moved to Houston and met Ben, a guy who worked the door of the bar where I waited tables. After two weeks, we were married. There is a lot you don't know about a person after only two weeks. We were both broken kids with no idea about how to be healed. After a traumatic late miscarriage and three babies, we divorced. Regardless, I know that Ben had loved me when he asked me to marry him. I don't regret our children or the life we had; I only regret that I didn't know then what I know now about marriage.

After my divorce from Ben, I began drinking heavily. I started sleeping around again just as I had as a teenager, only this time I was sleeping with gang members who were dangerous. I didn't care. I was more self-destructive than ever. I wasn't involved with my kids, which was hardest on my oldest son since he was becoming a teen at the time. I was in and out of jail.

It all stopped in May 2007, when I learned that Homer, my best friend at the time, died. In my grief, I decided to start over. I packed what I could in the trunk of my car, loaded up my kids, and headed to Austin. Ben was there. We tried—and failed—to reconcile.

In 2008, I got a message on MySpace from my old boyfriend Stacey Adams, who was then in Iraq. We moved in together when he came home and bought a beautiful house in the suburbs, with a fence, a huge backyard, and trees. We even got a dog. The American Dream. We have been together ever since.

Part of what comes with the American Dream is going to church. I knew that; so did Stacey. For a reason that I still can't explain, we both identified as Catholic. We began going to the nearest Catholic Church. Not regularly, but when we could, such as when the Cowboys or the Texans weren't playing at noon.

The first time I entered the church, I felt out of place. A shiver went up my spine, and I heard a whisper in my head saying, "You do not belong here." Then there was the sign on the door that said that if you weren't dressed appropriately, you would be asked to leave. I looked down at my shirt, which showed a lot of cleavage. I realized that probably it was inappropriate, but instead of leaving, which was my first impulse, I walked in, daring anyone to ask me to leave. If they had tried to kick me out, I would have made the biggest scene (I had been kicked out of a lot of bars in my life; it was never pretty); and then I would have told as many people as possible how stupid that church was. (They let me stay.)

Stacey and I were spending a lot of money going out, drinking, and having a good time. We went to swingers' clubs and lived in ways that I never would've imagined when I was a sweet little Baptist girl carrying her Bible around school, trying to get people to know Jesus. Ours was a wildly disordered way of life, but Stacey didn't hurt me the way so many other men had. To me, this was a win.

After a year or so, though, I started to feel that something was missing. I didn't know what exactly, but I started asking Stacey to prove to me that he loved me.

Soon, Stacey returned to Afghanistan for a few reasons, one being that we were fighting a lot. I wanted to get married, but he wasn't ready for that; and also, we were broke. He said that if we were ever to get married, it would have to be in the Catholic Church. I'm convinced he said that, thinking that I would never take the classes needed for me to get my sacraments, but he claims that isn't the case.

Well, I showed him because I did go to RCIA (the Rite of Christian Initiation of Adults) — but only to get Stacey to marry me.

I never intended to be Catholic.

Not really.

I mean, I already considered myself as Catholic as I was going to get, but I was not ever going to get behind banning birth control or abortion.

Nope. Not me.

The first class shocked me. A short Mexican man got up and started talking about God's love. I had never in my life heard a Catholic talk about how much God loves us. Not only that; he talked about Jesus as if Jesus were alive and he knew Jesus personally. Again, I had never seen a Catholic do that.

A second teacher finished the presentation saying, "God loves you more than you think He does. No matter what you have done, how far you've gone from Him, He loves you, and He wants you to come back to Him."

He said that with tears in his eyes, his voice shaky and with such conviction that it shook me to my core. When I left that class, I thought, "That man doesn't know it, but he's not Catholic; he's Baptist."

I sat in my car crying for about twenty minutes because I knew that what he had said was true. I had heard it before in the First Baptist Church in Kenedy, Texas.

I still was not ready to accept all those teachings on marriage, sexuality, and reproductive rights. While I was going through RCIA, I argued about every single one of those teachings.

For my first Confession, I walked into the office of a brand-new priest named Fr. Jonathan. I was very angry, very hard of heart, and very much living in a place of woundedness from my abuse as a child. The first thing that came out of my mouth was, "I can't be Catholic; I refuse to hate gay people." His response was to tell me that if I ever found that the Catholic Church taught that it was okay to hate gay people—or anyone else, for that matter—then I was right and I shouldn't become Catholic.

We talked about a lot of other things that day, including my abuse. In time, he taught me how to read the *Catechism* and papal documents. He also introduced me to St. John Paul II's theology of the body. I learned a lot and very fast.

Many things led Stacey and me to Rome during Holy Week 2010. We spent thirteen amazing days there. I was all set to enter the Catholic Church that Easter, but I was still not convinced about some of the Church's teachings. Stacey and I were in Rome together, sharing a hotel room and having sex.

For the first time in my life since I had started having sex, I felt guilty about it. I thought it was just typical Catholic guilt. What did it matter? We wanted to get married. In fact, we tried to elope in Rome. Let me just say that Rome is not Vegas, especially during Lent.

I went to Confession at St. Peter's and confessed to having sex outside of marriage and other things. I was sure the priest was going to tell me that I was not meant to be Catholic and I should try a different faith.

That's not what happened. I received so much mercy, kindness, and love from that confessor — just as I had from everyone during my RCIA process, even though I was always so sure that they were going to kick me out at any moment ... but that moment never came.

After Confession, I went back to our hotel room and sat on the floor with the *Catechism* open to a section about marriage. I came across this quote:

> I have taken you in my arms, and I love you, and I prefer you to my life itself. For the present life is nothing, and my most ardent dream is to spend it with you in such a way that we may be assured of not being separated in the life reserved for us.... I place your love above all things, and nothing would be more bitter or painful to me than to be of a different mind than you.

That quote spoke to everything in me that had been searching for love my entire life. In that passage, St. John Chrysostom described what I had been seeking in all the relationships, porn, swingers' clubs, one-night stands, failed marriage, and other dead ends of my life. I hungered for the kind of love that he said was proper in Catholic marriage. I didn't want anything short of it, and I was not willing to compromise on it ever again.

After an encounter with Christ on the Holy Stairs in Rome, Stacey felt the same way. We decided that we would do everything we could to get married in the Church once he was home from Afghanistan.

On our last day in Rome, we went on a walk down an ancient road near our hotel. It was a beautiful afternoon in the Roman countryside. Tradition has it that this is the road St. Peter took when he escaped from prison. He ran into the risen Christ on it. Jesus told him to go back to Rome, which he did, and he was martyred there.

As we walked down that road, I saw what seemed to be a white cloud coming our way. The few cars and people started to move out of the way, so we waited to see what was coming. Then Stacey said, "I think it's a herd of sheep."

When we had landed in Rome, I'd told Stacey that I wanted to see a herd of sheep because I had no idea why Jesus was so obsessed with them. As the sheep passed us, playing and following the shepherd, I stared at that dusty old man, who looked as if he had stepped straight out of the Bible. I saw a familiar gentle smile on his face, the gentle smile you see on pictures of Jesus.

With tears rolling down my face I looked at the sheep, and one of them looked right back at me, and I knew right then that there was nothing God wouldn't do for me. I also knew that I wasn't there by accident.

That's when I decided that even if I didn't agree, I would follow all the teachings of the Catholic Church. I would never stop asking questions, but they would always be questions to figure out why the Church teaches what she does.

That day, in the middle of a herd of sheep, I gave my life to the Good Shepherd. He had pursued me, romanced me, and made it clear that I belonged to Him. Finally, I had fallen in love with Him.

I was Home.

I would like to say that my story ends there, that we lived happily ever after, but that would be a lie. There have been a lot of ups and downs in the six years since that day, which was the best day of my life.

My husband and I have stood vigil as his dad died; we have prayed at the casket of his best friend; and we have watched his aunt spread the ashes of his grandmother, who was like a second mom to him.

Stacey battles wartime post-traumatic stress disorder; I have been in therapy for three years to face the trauma of my childhood. We have gone broke; our lights have been shut off; and as I type this, our houses is in foreclosure.

Ten months ago, I sat next to the bed of my beloved tio Roy as he took his last breath. It was by far one of the hardest things that I've ever done. It made me feel as if I were being ripped away from God. Tio Roy was one of the few people who always had my back. I always knew that I had a place to go when life got hard.

He and my tia were always there for me. As he lay in the hospital dying, my tia led us all in praying Rosary after Rosary for him. She gave us a bottle of holy water from San Juan to bless him with. During his funeral Mass, she was a pillar of strength for the rest of us when we should have been comforting her.

Just two weeks ago, I sat by my tia's bedside as she took her last breath. She taught us to mourn by leaning on God and to live by leaning on God. She taught us always to turn to Jesus in prayer and the sacraments.

Even as I write this, I am not sure how I am doing. One minute I'm at peace, and the next, tears won't stop flowing. But I will say that even though I've not felt the presence of God much these last few months, He has made it clear that He is with me. Even if it is by the weirdest means possible, He is still breaking through my deafness.

This is what the Catholic Faith looks like when it is lived out. When other people see us, they notice something different about us and about where we seek our strength. They see that we know Someone they don't and that it isn't just talk, but that we are living out what we say we believe.

What God has done for me He wants to do for you.

He loves you more than you think He does.

No matter what you've done or how far you've gone from Him, He is waiting for you to come home to Him.

LETICIA OCHOA ADAMS is a writer who resides with her husband and family near Austin, Texas. She is a regular contributor to the *Jennifer Fulwiler Show* on the Catholic Channel (Sirius XM channel 129) and is available for speaking events.

WWW.LETIADAMS.COM
LETICIAOADAMS@GMAIL.COM

FR. RYAN AND THE WOMEN'S CLINIC

LEILA MILLER

When I was a teen, my mom quietly gave me a large secular book on sex. She had stuck into its pages a cutout from our parish bulletin, which was an exhortation to save sex for marriage, something I already understood and accepted as the morally correct position. I understood (and still appreciate) that my mom's aim was to provide me with knowledge of all aspects of human sexuality and biology, with the reminder that sex was for marriage.

The book itself was thorough and explicit, and it included many detailed pencil illustrations. I was fascinated—both compelled and repelled—by its wide-ranging, morally neutral contents, from masturbation and homosexuality to contraception and abortion. My friends and I would furtively flip through it when they came over, alternately giggling and recoiling at the things we saw and read.

Between the poor catechesis and the pull of the culture as I got older, my will became weak. Essentially, I held a Christian worldview in my intellect, but exempted myself from living it out. After initial resistance, I eventually stepped off the moral path and became more and more complacent with my own serious sin.

I was comfortable and enjoying life on my own terms, convinced by my own self-importance that "God understands me" and all was well. I was a "good person," after all! Yes, I was willfully, knowingly transgressing the moral law, but didn't I pray every night, perfunctorily, "God, please forgive my sins"? Surely that covered it. Surely that was enough for God!

Once I got my driver's license, I fell into a weekly routine that perfectly illustrates the contradiction of those years. Sunday-morning Mass with my parents was boring, so every Sunday evening I drove myself to the beautiful (and trendy) candlelight Mass at a nearby parish. I would sing, pray, and march right up to receive Communion like everyone else.

As soon as I got back from Mass, I would go to my room, settle in with a bowl of sunflower seeds, and tune into *Sexually Speaking*, a radio call-in show hosted by the wildly popular sex therapist Dr. Ruth Westheimer. Dr. Ruth was a spunky, diminutive grandma figure with a thick German accent who dished out explicit sexual advice that would make your hair curl. It was high entertainment for this high school girl, and I loved my Sunday-night ritual.

Yes, I was appalled by much of what she said (promiscuity, homosexual acts, and abortion were all A-OK), but I remained a faithful listener. I can't count how many times she chirpily sent off a young caller with, "Rrremember! Yoos a condom!" Her academic degrees and celebrity status created the illusion of legitimate authority—and gave cover to anyone wishing to ditch traditional sexual morality for a more "progressive," hedonistic option.

By that time, I was already immersed in sexual sin. When I started down the road of sexual activity, I prided myself on not going "all the way." After all, although there was a lot of promiscuity and sex among teens back in the '80s, there was still a general understanding that sex was, ideally, meant for marriage. Even in a public high school, that ideal was respected, if not followed.

Once I opened the door to unchastity, however, I remember being incredibly frustrated at how long I would have to wait for marriage to have "real" sex. I had to get through the rest of high school and all of college before that could happen! I was annoyed and incredulous. Of course, had I possessed the habit of virtue and been chaste, the notion of "waiting" would not have seemed nearly as daunting. Still and all, and despite all my sinful acts, I was determined not to engage in the "full" marital act until, well, marriage. I was committed to that much (or that little), until the day that my boyfriend, who had convinced me to smoke pot and drink a little one night, decided we would have sex.

Neither one of us was sober, and one of us protested and said no, but there you have it. It was done, and there was no going back. Sober the next day, my boyfriend felt bad about things and thought we should break up, believing that would make things better for me. Of course, that's not at all how the mind of a young girl thinks. For me, a breakup would be the worst thing in the world. In fact, now that the deed was done, we *had* to stay together, because in my mind, at least, we were forever bonded. We had to get married one day.

Since waiting for marriage was no longer an option in my mind, I needed to find a way to get through the rest of high school and four years of college without getting pregnant. I was utterly against abortion, and I knew that a child deserved to be born into a family, to a married mother and father. But I had to find some way to facilitate my sin of premarital sex. What to do, then, until that far-off wedding day?

One of my best friends had also started having sex with the boyfriend she assumed she'd eventually marry. She and I decided to go to Planned Parenthood and get on birth control pills. After all, guys didn't like to use condoms because condoms reduced their pleasure during sex, so it was clearly our job to get our young, growing bodies on hormones that would derail our fertility and makes us perpetually available.

My friend was not Catholic, so contraception was not something she felt was a moral issue (unlike premarital sex, which she was personally against, but which she justified). As for me, I had a vague notion that contraception was not technically allowed for Catholics. I remember I had snottily challenged my dad about it at some point — "Why does the Catholic Church say that birth control is wrong, anyway?" — and he didn't have an answer. He suggested that I "ask someone who knows about these things," but, of course, I never did. I was not passionate about finding an answer, and I would not have known whom to ask anyway.

FR. RYAN AND THE WOMEN'S CLINIC

So, on a sunny day in the summer of '84, my friend and I, both minors, drove ourselves to a Planned Parenthood clinic in Tucson, Arizona. I wrote my name on the sign-in sheet and saw another teen's name there from earlier in the day, a pretty, raven-haired cheerleader from a nearby high school. *Gosh*, I thought, *I wonder how many other girls I know are patients here!*

As my friend and I sat in the plastic seats in the reception area, we were a bit anxious; we were doing something "forbidden" and rebellious, and we were worried that we'd be found out. We silently exchanged nervous smiles, and I was grateful that I had a friend with me to share what seemed like an adult adventure! Our parents must never know what we were doing, and we trusted, correctly, that the Planned Parenthood workers would keep our little secret.

In fact, there was a whole protocol for keeping parents in the dark. When the receptionist learned that I was underage and wanted to keep all this confidential, she said I'd be designated a "CODE MINDY." There were no cell phones back then, and the woman explained that if a clinic worker had to call my house for any reason, she would identify herself as "Mindy," as if she were just some school friend of mine. So if I heard there was a call from "Mindy," I would know the call was from Planned Parenthood, and a parent who answered the phone would be none the wiser.

After giving me this reassuring explanation of the plan, the receptionist took out a rubber stamp and pounded a red-inked "CODE MINDY" on my file. I can still see it in my mind's eye today, over thirty years later. I was a CODE MINDY, and so was my friend.

Next up was the internal gynecological exam, which was nerve-racking, as it was my first. It went quickly, and I can't remember the female adult (a doctor? a nurse?) asking me anything about my situation, to ascertain if I were in danger or to talk me about the physical, emotional, or psychological risks of being a sexually active, unmarried teen. It was obvious to me even at the time that her job was simply to fulfill the requirements that would get me the prescription I wanted.

I also have no recollection of being informed of the myriad risks of being on hormonal birth control: everything from mood swings, depression, and weight gain to death, due to a stroke or blood clots. I'm certain I was never told that the pill works by tricking the body into thinking it is continually, endlessly pregnant, and that sometimes, if a child is conceived while his mother is on the pill, the drug works as an abortifacient, sweeping away the new baby before the mother even knows she is pregnant.

The Planned Parenthood workers were adults, of course, but they acted like adolescents. They were like an immature, irresponsible friend: a willing accomplice to a seedy, dishonorable deed that must be kept from parents. Under the pretense of "health" and "choice," these workers were, consciously or not, facilitating the corruption of young girls. Grown-ups failed me.

Ironically, I walked out of that building feeling more like a grown-up than ever before. I had an important secret. I was mature. I was also aware that what I was doing was morally wrong, but, oh well, "God understands." After the first sin, conscience finds it easier to justify others. My friend and I giggled and clutched our brown paper bags that contained our first month's supply of birth control pills! This sure would make things a lot easier for our boyfriends, whom we wanted to please. Indeed, they were happy with what we had done.

A little over a year later, I arrived at Boston College, thousands of miles from home. Still believing myself to be a devout Catholic, I had chosen a Jesuit university to better my chances of finding and marrying a Catholic husband in case my hometown boyfriend left me permanently. In fact, he had been cheating for quite some time, and I was not much more than an afterthought and an occasional plaything to him. I was still a teenaged girl "in love," though, and thanks to the birth control pills, I was always available to him when we were in the same town.

Because my boyfriend was not interested in commitment or monogamy, I alternated between brokenheartedness or anger when he cheated and hope when he came back, all the while dating other guys in the interim. I was certainly not living a life of chastity, but I prided myself on the fact that I was not doing nearly as much bad stuff as others; I was quite self-satisfied about that.

Although the culture at Boston College in the late '80s was not as depraved as we see in colleges today, an authentic Catholic ethos was already gone. A striking golden-eagle sculpture stands mounted on a large pillar at the entrance to the campus, and the first inside joke that every freshman heard was that "the eagle will fly when a virgin graduates from BC." I thought it was funny but also appalling; part of me was still right-thinking enough to be disturbed. Just as in high school, I was living in contradiction—a state that was mirrored by campus life in general: although the college took a proper and even courageous pro-life stand, under the guise of "women's health services," the student newspaper ran ads for nearby abortion clinics. Many students assured me that at times and contrary to school policy, nurses in the student health center secretly referred students for abortions.

During my sophomore year, I had a pregnancy scare. The thought of abortion never entered my mind, even though I knew that having a child out of wedlock would upend my life. My wayward boyfriend was not in town, so I begged one of my girlfriends to accompany me to one of the "women's clinics" that I had seen advertised so many times; I was only going for the "free pregnancy test" they constantly promoted. My friend was not happy, as she was strongly pro-life and wanted no part of a clinic like this. Ultimately, she put aside her discomfort and disgust and accompanied me to the worst place I've ever been, even to this day.

I can't remember how I convinced myself to walk into that place. Did I tell myself that this was a health clinic only, where they did not perform abortions? I don't know. All I know is that when I walked into that place, it was like walking into the cold and dark of hell. The women in the seats had a death pall on their faces, as if the life had been drained out of them. The receptionist was stony and gray.

The woman who took me back to the double bank of dingy stalls for the urine sample was as pallid and mechanical as the others, and I remember wondering, *What is wrong with all these people?* It was downright funereal. In the course of writing this piece, I asked my friend to recall our trek to that clinic, an event she had all but forgotten. We had not discussed it in thirty years, and yet she remembers the place as "somber, sad, and scary," describing it as "cold, sterile, and unfeeling."

With a flat affect, the dreary woman informed me that my pregnancy test was negative. Relieved, I hurried back to my friend, who had been left in that dreadful waiting room, and we flew out of there into the fresh air.

My poor friend was upset. "I am never going back to a place like that ever again!" I finally realized what those women were there for, and that the pall of death was real. A shiver went down my spine, and I apologized to my friend as we fled the area, trying to shake that doleful experience from our souls. Making a sacramental confession, which would have accomplished my redemption, never entered my mind.

Fr. Ryan, one of the few professors I truly admired at Boston College, taught a Catholic Theology of Marriage class that I chose precisely because of my desire to marry and have a family after I completed my degree. I knew that academically and professionally I could be very successful, but my deepest desire was for hearth and home.

In Fr. Ryan's class, I heard for the first time in my life the reasons the Church is opposed to contraception. He taught about the two intrinsic aspects of sex, the unitive (bonding) and the procreative (babies), and how artificially separating the two, or accepting one and discarding the other, leads to untold social, physical, and spiritual crises. I loved the theology he explained, but the argument that really spoke to me was the natural law argument—the idea that everything should be understood and used according to its nature. If a thing is used according to its nature or design, there will be flourishing and right order. If a thing is used against its nature and design, there will be decline and disorder.

Fr. Ryan taught basic truths that I never knew as a woman, including the fact that we women could read the signs of our fertility, and that God built in more nonfertile than fertile days in our cycles. None of this was rocket science; it was inherent in my very nature, and yet no one had ever told me or my peers any of this. I felt cheated. The good priest even laid out the symbiotic connection between contraception and abortion, which I had never considered before. Everything he said made sense to me. It was all logical, reasonable, clear.

I was baffled that no one else in the class seemed to "buy it" or to care at all. Overwhelmingly, they despised the old priest and made fun of him behind his back, but I admired him. Now, let's be clear: in my habit of sin, I was certainly not about to change my ways at that point (I barely even went to Mass anymore), but I thought I might try that natural family planning thing someday, maybe a few years after I got married.

Fr. Ryan explained for me the section of life's puzzle that represented human sexuality. Although this did not complete the whole picture for me, it would be instrumental years later, when I was turning back to God's grace and finally seeking His will above my own. My intellect was in good working order, but my will was still way out of whack. I was stubborn and lazy, and I needed the whole picture to be revealed before my heart would be moved to act on what good Fr. Ryan taught.

In my junior year of college I finally cut ties with my on-and-off boyfriend for good, and then cried on the shoulder of my good friend Dean, a Jewish agnostic boy whom I met in DC during a college exchange semester. We started dating, and within a couple of weeks we were sleeping together. Two years later we were married in the Catholic Church. I had marched down the aisle in a state of mortal sin, still believing myself devout.

Dean and I never considered the idea that God was part of the planning of our family size, and we decided to have three children quickly and be done, so that we would be free to travel and have fun in our forties! It was the perfect plan!

In just a few years, we had three children.

Having a fourth was unthinkable, of course, but what I didn't anticipate was my "mourning" the fourth child I would never know. I had so loved nursing and cuddling my three babies. I loved watching them grow, getting to know each one uniquely, and falling in love all over again when the next unrepeatable, irreplaceable child was born. I understood that they were gifts from God. I knew that a fourth child would be as amazing, as beloved, as perfectly suited for our family as the first three.

And so, for a brief time, I indulged the melancholy daydream of my fourth child who would never be, and then I let that child go. It was time to permanently sterilize our marriage.

I was such a failed Catholic at the time that I remember telling Dean, "Hey, it's against my religion to get sterilized, so you have to get a vasectomy!" I thought that I was funny, but he agreed that it made the most sense. At the time, some friends were making the same decision. After two children, they were "done" and ready for the husband to "get fixed"—an ironic euphemism, indeed.

Our friends made an appointment for a consultation with the urologist who would do the procedure, and, assuming they liked the doctor, Dean would schedule with him next, along with a third couple planning the same. Looking back, I see God intervening in the form of an unhygienic doctor: our friends had been horrified that the urologist had failed to wash his hands between patients, and they left the consultation grossed out and without an appointment for the vasectomy.

Providentially, this event coincided with the beginning of my turn back to the Faith, which put the thoughts of sterilization on hold. Praise be to God, none of the three men who were going to get a vasectomy went through with it, and, in total, seven more children were born to three couples because that doctor did not wash his hands that day.

During my "reversion" process, I was initially going to leave the Catholic Church and join my friend Kim's evangelical Bible Church. She had been raised Episcopalian, rejected Christianity in college, and had recently emerged from paganism and radical feminism. My mother (a Catholic convert) told me, "Find out what you are leaving before you leave," and followed up by handing me the first book on Catholic apologetics I had ever seen, *Catholicism and Fundamentalism* by Karl Keating. I was overwhelmed with all the truths I had never learned. Over the course of the next year and through our friendly but intense debates, Kim's studies and the grace of Christ led her to the Catholic Church, with Patrick Madrid's *Surprised by Truth* instrumental in laying waste to her Protestant suppositions.

While Kim and I investigated and worked through doctrinal and moral issues, the beauty and consistency of Catholic teaching left me more and more awestruck. What Fr. Ryan had taught me years before came together seamlessly with what I was currently learning, and suddenly *all* the pieces of the puzzle fell into place. I saw the big picture—the historical, logical, biblical, and spiritual truth of Catholicism.

The discovery was miraculous, transcendent, with the Holy Trinity at the heart of everything, the source of all creation, the end of every desire. From the first book of Scripture to the last, from the beginning of salvation history to its culmination, the language and understanding is essentially nuptial. Christ the Eternal Bridegroom fully loves His Bride (the Church—us!), holding nothing back. In heaven, at the consummation of history, Christ's beloved will partake in the Wedding Feast of the Lamb, and perfect union with Jesus will be achieved. Earthly marriage is a reflection and foretaste of spiritual marriage with God in heaven.

Just as my impoverished view and disordered practice of human sexuality could never satisfy, so my patchy, fragmented understanding of Catholicism would never again satisfy. A colorful, sweeping, welcoming vista now opened before me, and I rushed forward to enter, delighting like a child! I didn't want to contracept anymore, not physically with my husband, and not spiritually with God. I didn't want to hold back any part of myself with either one.

And yet ... how could I expect my non-Christian husband to give up contraception in our marriage? I knew that this sea change would transform our marriage for the better, but how to convince him? After all, we were still in our twenties, and two decades of fertility loomed ahead of us. Our carefully controlled future would dissolve into uncertainty and mystery. For me, that mystery was enticing. That fourth child I mourned: would I one day know him after all? Joy filled my soul at the knowledge that I could, with God's permission, reject our utilitarian, materialistic culture and embrace the mind and freedom of Christ! I prayed that my husband would see the beauty of the Truth.

Enter another great mercy. While Kim and I walked our spiritual journey together, Dean overheard my months of discoveries and excitement about the Church. One night, as I explained how Christ was foretold in the Hebrew Scriptures, he recognized Jesus prefigured in those prophecies, with Psalm 22 particularly convicting him. From there, the connections between Judaism and Catholicism came easily. Whereas before, Dean had not fully understood nor believed his Jewish faith, he now embraced it all as true. To become Catholic was to recognize his Messiah and become a "completed Jew." The Church was the continuation of Judaism, and the New Covenant was God's long-planned culmination of the Old.

Dean's deepened connection to his Jewishness made the contraception question easy. The purest, most traditional forms of Judaism greatly value marriage and procreation—love leading to life!—and contraception was and is heavily frowned upon, if not outright forbidden. This reverence for the gift of fertility in both Judaism and Catholicism made sense to Dean and confirmed for him the veracity of Church teaching. The puzzle pieces were put into place for him as well, and now we both beheld the same beautiful picture.

We stopped using contraception more than twenty years ago, and we've never regretted it. On my thirtieth birthday, Dean was baptized, confirmed, and received his First Eucharist at the Easter Vigil Mass. Exactly one year later, our fourth child was baptized. He was and is as perfect and special as I always dreamed he would be. Over the next years, we welcomed our fifth, sixth, seventh, and eighth children—all loved and wanted, all good and perfect gifts for our family.

At the same time, our worldview has become wildly expansive and perfectly harmonious, and we now have a firm foundation from which to see and evaluate everything around us as it comes. The clarity that the Church provides is the calm in the storm of a world that spirals further and further away from reality itself.

The puzzle came together for us two decades ago, long before the era of ubiquitous, virtual-reality porn, of genderless marriage, of men "becoming" women, and of "gender fluidity." Yet as acceptance of these lifestyles and sins overwhelmed our culture with shocking force and rapidity, we were able to understand why they were fundamentally wrong and harmful.

The full picture comes with great grace. Dean and I have raised our eight children with all the puzzle pieces in place, and they have avoided the sexual pitfalls of their parents. Our three oldest children are in holy, fruitful marriages. To God be the glory!

Millions of souls, however, are disoriented, lost, adrift, trying to make sense of new movements that contradict basic science and biology, denying human nature itself. Out of a false sense of compassion or fear or social shaming, many go along with or even affirm the false ideologies of sexual "progressives"—even when they know on some level that none of it makes sense.

Unless we go back to the beginning (literally, "con-ception") and stop going against the beginning (literally, "*contra*-ception"), we will continue in anxiety and fear. We will fight our own human nature and wonder why we are so lost and afraid, and why our lives and souls are filled with chaos and disorder.

Isn't it funny that we search for pleasure and love and happiness in sinful, distorted forms of sexuality, and that instead of joy we eventually find the "sad and scary, cold and unfeeling" darkness (surely a hallmark of hell itself) that I experienced in that "women's clinic" years ago? When we encounter our brothers and sisters who live in such disordered confusion, we must gently, prudently, *courageously* hand them the pieces to the puzzle that they lack. We must be Christ—and Fr. Ryan—to others. There is not a soul on earth who was not made to know and love the Truth.

As I have mercifully learned, the Church is a gentle Mother and a wise Teacher. When sex and life are lived in harmony with our own human nature, we lose our existential angst. The peace and joy of Christ replaces our anxiety and fear. This is the gift! This is freedom! And I praise God every day that He pursued me until every piece was in place, and I fell safely into His arms.

LEILA MILLER is the author of *Raising Chaste Catholic Men: Practical Advice, Mom to Mom*, and *Primal Loss: The Now-Adult Children of Divorce Speak*. She writes the blog *Little Catholic Bubble*, where her "other" reversion story can be found. Leila is wife to Dean, mother to eight, and grandmother to an ever-expanding number of grandbabies. She and her family live in Phoenix.

LITTLECATHOLICBUBBLE@GMAIL.COM

FROM ONE HOLOCAUST TO ANOTHER

CHRIS AUBERT

In Paris in 1941, the Nazis arrested my father, his sister, and his parents. They were all Polish Jews. Although my father was then only fifteen, he was already a gifted violinist. In July of 1942, the Nazis put him on a train to the Auschwitz-Birkenau concentration camp in Poland. Upon his arrival, they tattooed on his left forearm his prisoner number: 49948. Then, because of his violin skills, they assigned him to the Birkenau Orchestra, which required him to entertain the SS troops.

Two months later, the Nazis sent my father's parents to Auschwitz-Birkenau as well. Anna was likely also sent there, but the records are sketchy.

The Birkenau Orchestra was forced to entertain the SS troops during the death marches the condemned prisoners took from their barracks to the gas chambers. My father led many of these marches, including the one that brought his own father and mother to their death.

As the Russians advanced on Poland, the Nazis blew up much of the Auschwitz-Birkenau camp and took the remaining twelve thousand to sixteen thousand prisoners west to internment camps in Germany. My father had to march for sixteen days before ending up at Buchenwald in central Germany. He survived Buchenwald by continuing to entertain the SS troops in their orchestra.

When General Patton's army liberated Europe, my father, like many Jewish Holocaust survivors, sought a better life in America. Fearing another holocaust, he masked his Jewish identity by adopting a French persona and changing his name from Henry Hochberg to Henri Aubert. (He chose the name Aubert because of his fondness for the Aubert Lutherie Bridge and Instrument Company, which manufactured his violin.) In America, he met my Catholic mother and married her, and I was born in New York City on May 19, 1957.

Despite his Jewish faith, my father wanted to make sure that nobody knew that I had Jewish roots. Hoping to protect me from another holocaust, he urged my mother to name me Christian Joseph, but they settled on Christopher. Despite my father's best efforts, a holocaust—an American Holocaust—would overwhelm me later in my life.

When I was two years old, my parents divorced; when I was fourteen, my father died. Meanwhile, when I was five, my mother, whose Catholic Faith was not very important to her, married another Jewish man and converted to Judaism for him. I was raised Jewish and bar mitzvahed in 1970.

We were a Jewish version of Christmas and Easter Christians. For the most part, the High Holy Days were the only times we went to temple. The last time I was formally in temple was for my bar mitzvah. There was no strong reason for this; religion was just not an important part of my upbringing.

I graduated from high school in 1975 and entered Tulane University, which is in the very Catholic city of New Orleans, but has a large percentage of northeastern Jews. Despite this diversity, I found no real religious life at Tulane and lived a largely secular life. Organized religion had no place in my world: like many young people in that era, I was the center of my own universe.

I was also the king of rationalizations. If I did something wrong, I easily justified it: "Hey, everyone does it and no one gets hurt, so what's the big deal?" I used this excuse for guiltless partying of all kinds, frequent indiscriminate sex, and many other things for which today I'm ashamed and embarrassed.

After graduating from Tulane in 1979, I went to work as a sportscaster and producer at WWL, a fifty-thousand-watt powerhouse radio station in New Orleans with a nationwide signal at night. Although the station was owned by Loyola University and run by the Jesuits, when the station's regular programming ended at 8 p.m., we ran prerecorded religious programming until midnight, mostly of the Protestant variety, including Marvin Gorman, Jimmy Swaggart, and others.

One of my many jobs was to spin these tapes for four hours a night, every night. I paid little attention to what these preachers said, other than thinking they were kooks. You see, I was still the king of my own universe; nothing sunk in, not even by accident.

Once I realized I wasn't going to be the next superstar network sportscaster, I quit the radio business, entering Tulane Law School in 1981. I had a few simple goals: to be rich and powerful and to own the biggest, most expensive Mercedes-Benz they made. I graduated from Tulane Law School in 1984 and took a job at a large, prestigious corporate law firm in New Orleans. I continued to pursue my secular goals. There was no reason to change, especially since wealth, power, and a big Mercedes were now within reach. When I wasn't working, I chased girls, usually juggling two or three girlfriends at a time.

In 1985, I broke up with one girl just because it was time to move on to another. Several weeks later, after we had not talked at all, she started calling me. I dodged her ever-more-frequent calls by letting the answering machine get them. As far as I was concerned, we had nothing to talk about.

One evening, I accidentally picked up the phone before the machine got it. It was she, calling to tell me she had something important to talk to me about. I resisted, but she persisted. Eventually, she persuaded me to go to meet her for what I was convinced would be an attempt to resurrect the relationship.

When I got there, this girl—who had not been a serious girlfriend—sat me on the couch and matter-of-factly blurted out, "Chris, I'm pregnant." Before I could absorb the news, she added, "and I want to get an abortion."

At that time for me, marriage was not in the cards, either with her or anyone else. Marriage would have blocked my path to money and power ... and that Mercedes-Benz. So I gladly agreed with her decision to abort, using the same excuses we hear today: "It's just a blob of unviable tissue"; "It's her body, and she can do with it what she pleases"; "I'm too young"; "I'm not ready to have children"; and that old standby, "This is America, and our Supreme Court says abortion is legal!"

She was relieved at my response and asked if I wanted to go with her to the doctor that weekend. I declined because this abortion was a total nonevent for me. I just wrote a check, dropping it off at her house the next day when I knew she wasn't home; and that was the end of it.

I'm ashamed to admit that I never gave that event, or that girl, much more than a passing thought over the next few years.

My serial dating continued unchanged. In 1991, I got another girl pregnant. Although she was a steady girlfriend, marriage was still not an option; I remained caught up in my selfish life. We talked about what to do with this "little problem," and I happily agreed with her suggestion to have an abortion.

This time, though, I went to the clinic, sat in the waiting room, paid the bill, and took her to lunch afterward. At lunch, we didn't talk much about what we'd just done. Mainly, I remember the silence. Although I had freely and even eagerly agreed to this second abortion, something about it felt wrong, but I didn't know what. I also began thinking again about the first abortion. Nonetheless, apart from an occasional awkward feeling, they had no lasting effect on me.

About this same time, I heard someone call abortion "the American Holocaust." As the son of a Holocaust survivor, I was struck by the use of that word. I grew curious about why abortion was such a big issue for so many people. Without much thought, I had always accepted secular society's claim that abortion was strictly a woman's health issue. I had agreed to the two abortions because, as I saw it at the time, a baby wasn't being killed; rather, a woman was just exercising her right to choose what to do with her body.

Why wouldn't I think this way?

Everywhere I turned, abortion was portrayed as the enlightened position in tough situations faced by women who just wanted autonomy over their bodies.

It never occurred to me to consider what God thought about abortion. In fact, I had no real understanding of God or truth. As for the Bible, I don't think I owned one. I couldn't tell you the difference between the Old Testament and the New Testament: I had never even read the book! I didn't know if it was history, fantasy, fiction, or something else. When people asked me my religion, I'd say Jewish, but that was more out of habit and history than any set of beliefs. In fact, I didn't even know what Jews believed. How embarrassing for a man with two advanced degrees.

Jesus? I didn't know if He was fictional or real, what people thought He had done, or why they thought it important. When a Christian asked me if I was "saved," I thought, "What does that mean? Saved from what?"

A year or so after that second abortion, I met Rhonda, a cradle Catholic from New Orleans. I started learning from her a little more about Jesus Christ, Catholicism, and all the things that go with it. Rhonda is a wonderful, beautiful woman. In those days, I was still pro-choice, and Rhonda was, to a large extent, what too many other Catholics are: faithful, but C.W.C. (Catholic when convenient). Nevertheless, through her I became acquainted with the basics of the Catholic Faith.

In June 1994, Rhonda and I married, and she got pregnant two months later. When she was about eight weeks pregnant, I saw for the first time in my life in the ultrasound waiting room a fetal development chart and was stunned by what it showed.

Before I could process this information, we were called into the ultrasound room. On the screen was that supposedly unviable tissue mass moving around, right before my eyes. I couldn't believe it, and I pointed at the screen excitedly and said out loud, "I want to meet the person who says that's not a baby, because there is no doubt that's a baby!"

The light of truth—God's truth—had finally penetrated my blindness! Instantly, I understood the evil of abortion and was flooded with shame and sorrow for having been instrumental in the deaths of two of my own little babies.

Literally only minutes earlier I had been pro-choice; now I was pro-life. Now I saw that abortions are, indeed, the American Holocaust, very much like the one that my father survived and the one that he feared would come again.

I kept my new convictions to myself, though, mostly out of embarrassment and shame, feelings I had never before fully associated with abortion.

Our daughter Christine arrived in May 1995, and seeing her —this glorious miracle from God—convicted me even more.

The truth was now starkly clear: I had caused my first two children to be dismembered and thrown into a garbage can.

The majesty of Christine's tiny new life highlighted the poverty of my spiritual state. At one moment, I'd feel blessed by God's love, and the next, I'd feel empty and lost because I had hardly a clue about Him and His role in my life.

My relativism could not reconcile these extremes—particularly now that I saw clearly that there was truth, absolute truth, about abortion that proved relativism false.

But what does a New York Jew do with such confusion? Thankfully, my wife took charge in late 1996, enrolling me in the St. Peter parish RCIA program in Covington, Louisiana. By the grace of God, I entered the Catholic Church at the Easter Vigil Mass in 1997, just one day after God gave me a second miracle—my first son, Kyle.

Now that I was Catholic, I yearned to know more about my new Faith. So when a friend invited me to a Bible study class, I quickly accepted. It was led by a wonderful and kind "nondenominational" pastor, a man obviously on fire for his faith, and was attended by many fallen-away Catholics. At my first meeting, I was told that the group had only one rule: "We leave our denominational differences at the door, and go only by what the Bible says."

This sounded reasonable, so I started attending regularly. There were about ten guys in the group, two or three of whom were Catholic, and it was, honestly, great male fellowship.

In the first few months of this Bible study, discussions occasionally came up that, for reasons I could not explain, seemed a little off. I was hardly an expert on the Catholic Faith, but I would hear things that sounded inconsistent with what I understood the Catholic Church to teach.

I recall one person saying, "Matthew 23:9 says, 'Call no man father' — why do you Catholics call your priests Father when that goes directly against the Bible?" This made me uncomfortable because, after all, Matthew 23:9 did say just that. I let this comment slide without discussion or investigation, mainly because I didn't have a good response.

I recall a particularly troubling day when the leader discussed John 6: "He who eats my flesh and drinks my blood has eternal life.... My flesh is food indeed, and my blood is drink indeed" (vv. 54–55). The pastor said that here Jesus was speaking only figuratively. I thought, "Gee, I sure don't read it that way." I stayed silent, though, because he had a seminary degree, and I didn't have enough confidence in my knowledge of the Faith to discuss or debate the issue.

Later, I couldn't shake my confusion. Why did this pastor tell us that John 6 meant something figuratively, when it rather obviously — at least to me — read quite literally?

I decided that I couldn't accept this "nondenominational" teaching at face value, so I went to the *Catechism of the Catholic Church*. I quickly discovered that my pastor friend had a very different view of John 6 than did the Catholic Church.

As a lawyer, I know that words mean things. The words in John 6 were clear, but what was the truth they were conveying?

And as a lawyer, I need to know the truth, the whole truth, and nothing but the truth. As a budding antirelativist, I also knew that truth never contradicts truth. Thus, my pastor friend's belief and the Catholic Church's teaching on John chapter 6 could not both be true.

One of them was dead wrong.

But which one?

The question of whether the Eucharist was a cracker or Almighty God was surely not insignificant. How I could leave this "denominational difference" at the door? This was doubly troubling because future differences of interpretation were inevitable. I didn't know what to do, so I again decided to do nothing, mainly because I still did not know, for sure, who was right, or why.

As time went on, I continued to hear things in Bible study that sounded to me, as a rookie Catholic, to be clearly directed against the Catholic Church and her teachings. I see now that my Catholic Faith was being challenged.

The phrase "blind faith" does not fit me well. I could not accept these anti-Catholic views just because others held them, even if they knew more about Scripture. I had to learn for myself whether what they believed was true.

I compiled a list of the reasons my friends opposed the Church: call men father; denying that Jesus had brothers; worshipping Mary and statues; praying to dead people; purgatory; works righteousness; infant Baptism; adding books to the Bible; sinful popes; flat liturgy; and so on. I was determined to discover why my faith-filled friends disputed the Church's views on these matters and why some even left the Church because of them. Indeed, at the beginning of my inquiries, I assumed that they were right, and that I, too, should leave the Church, but I needed to prove that the Catholic Church was wrong, so I could in good conscience abandon what I had just joined.

My goal was to graduate to the "upper echelon of Christianity," as one of my closest ex-Catholic friends called his new faith.

What a failure I was.

First, I learned that virtually all the anti-Catholic beliefs I had heard were grossly exaggerated, or, worse, outright false. Accidentally or by design, my friends had created straw men and then attacked the straw men. They didn't know or understand the true teachings of the Catholic Church. Consequently, they weren't proving the Catholic Church wrong at all; they were exposing their own lack of knowledge or, worse, their intellectual dishonesty.

As I delved into the teachings of the Church, I began fully to comprehend—for the first time—biblical context, the difference between veneration and worship, the proper understanding of works in our salvation, the real meaning of papal infallibility, and all that goes with the majesty of Holy Mother Church.

I came to see the truth of Bishop Fulton Sheen's comment that "there are not over a hundred people in the United States who hate the Catholic Church. There are millions, however, who hate what they wrongly believe to be the Catholic Church."[1] So simple, yet so profound; and exactly what I had personally experienced.

---

[1] Quoted in Reverend Charles Mortimer Carty and Reverend Leslie Rumble, preface to *Radio Replies*, vols. 1–3 (N.p.: Catholic Way Publishing, 2015).

The more I studied, the more I found that the Catholic Church did, indeed, have a reasoned, thoughtful, coherent, and biblically solid theology that had been consistent from the time of Jesus on, and that had been accepted virtually unchallenged for fifteen hundred years, until the time of Martin Luther.

I came to see this clearly because, unlike my friends who had chosen to leave the Church for many different (and usually personal lifestyle) reasons, I did not approach the Bible or seek the truth with preconceived notions. I was open to the totality of the biblical and historical evidence, and when I looked at it without an agenda, the truth could hardly have been clearer.

In the last Bible study I ever went to, my pastor friend asked whether Baptism was necessary for salvation or was just symbolic. I responded, "Yes, Baptism is definitely necessary for salvation." He said that my belief was not biblical. I knew that it was, but I could not cite the passages, so I backed off. But only temporarily!

Later that day, I went before the Blessed Sacrament to read the *Catechism* and some other resources on Baptism. I then e-mailed my friend a lengthy analysis of the Catholic position based on two citations from the *Catechism*: John 3:5 ("Jesus answered, 'Truly, truly, I say to you, unless one is born of water and the Spirit, he cannot enter the kingdom of God'") and Mark 16:16 ("He who believes and is baptized will be saved"). My challenge to him was, "Explain to me why the Catholic Church is wrong on this."

He wrote me a lengthy response, claiming the Church did not properly interpret John 3:5, but he did not address Mark 16:16. When I called to his attention this apparent oversight, at first he didn't respond. When I reminded him a day or two later, he sidestepped the question twice more before eventually dismissing the question without an answer.

He avoided the question because he didn't have an answer to the question — and that's because there is no coherent answer.

So I invited my pastor friend to lunch and told him I would not be returning to Bible study. Seeing this as his last chance to save me from the Whore of Babylon and the Antichrist, he leveled many charges against the Church.

Thanks be to God, I now had confidence that the Church had heard all such attacks and had for each an answer that was thoughtful, profound, and true.

Second, I had become familiar with at least the first layer of the Church's multilayered teachings, so I could respond cogently to most anti-Catholic claims.

At that lunch, I left behind me any remaining doubt about Holy Mother Church and became a house built on firm ground, a seed planted in rich soil.

Time and again, I marvel at the treasure of the Holy Roman Catholic Church; time and again, my faith is comforted with truth.

God's goodness is awesome, particularly His ability to bring good out of evil. Without God's showering His love and grace on me after two abortions and giving me eyes to see and ears to hear, I don't think I would have learned the truth about the American Holocaust of abortion.

Without God's giving me the blessings of curiosity and skepticism, I would never have considered why people leave the

Church or have undertaken my misguided study to prove something wrong that could not be proven wrong.

For a long time after I found my true Faith, I was a warrior for truth, on fire for the Faith. Sometimes my zeal overwhelmed others. Now, when asked why I believe in the Catholic Church, my answer is simple: because it's true!

CHRIS AUBERT is a lawyer representing businesses and corporate entities in civil litigation. By avocation, he's a Catholic apologist, evangelist, and writer and for eighteen months was the host of the nationally syndicated talk show *Right Here, Right Now* on Immaculate Heart Radio. Chris has been featured in numerous media outlets including the *Los Angeles Times*, the Coming Home Network, Catholic Answers, the Catholic Channel, Closer Walk Ministries Television, Relevant Radio, *Envoy Magazine*, and *Legatus Magazine*. He is working on a book tentatively entitled *Real Men Don't Kill Their Kids*. Chris and his wife, Rhonda, live in Southlake, Texas, with their six children, ranging in age from twenty-two to six.

CHRIS@CHRISAUBERT.COM

CHRISAUBERT.COM

LITTLE MIRACLES LEADING FROM DEATH TO LIFE

DOREEN CAMPBELL

—∘ ᜒ ∘—

D eath is the life issue of all life issues.

This life doesn't make much sense if we don't have trust in what happens in the next one. This is my story about how much easier this life becomes when we receive God's assurance of eternal life. God came to this earth to show us the way back, and by His Cross and Resurrection we know that even in death He brings life.

—∘ ᜒ ∘—

December 14, 2008, the day it happened, began as a relatively typical day. My husband, Craig, was a firefighter and was teaching a class at the station that day. My two oldest kids, Cody and Kaydee, were home from college. My two youngest, Allee and Taylor, were very excited about having their siblings home because the house had been way too quiet since they left at the end of the summer. This would be the day we took our annual family Christmas pictures.

After a morning of catching up with Cody and Kaydee, the kids got ready to go to take the pictures. A few days earlier, I had spotted a beautiful tree that I knew would make a perfect backdrop. When we got there, my kids decided that climbing into the tree would make a much more interesting photo. After we took those photos, we went to a rock in front of a backdrop of gorgeous rolling hills.

I got another twenty-five pictures of my kids on that rock, and treasure each one of them. I captured moments that would make me smile later, remembering how much my kids loved each other and enjoyed spending time together.

By the time we got home and agreed on our favorite picture for the Christmas card, it was time to go to Mass. We always attended Mass together. That practice played an essential role in healing the wound that we were about to receive.

That day, the first extraordinary occurrence happened as we pulled into the church. Cody said, "Mom, if you were going to Church and you saw a stranger on the side of the road who needed help, would God want you to go to church and receive the Eucharist, or would He want you to stop and help the stranger?" Later, I would remember that question.

Decorating the house for the holidays followed Mass that night. My mom played the piano, and Taylor filled our home with her beautiful, faith-filled rendition of the song that would come back to bless us over and over again for years to come, including the day of the funeral: "Amazing Grace."

After we finished decorating, Craig went to bed because he had to teach the next day. My body was giving in to the long day, and I had to work in the morning, so I wanted to get to bed soon, too.

Mikey, Kaydee's boyfriend, was on his way to our home and he and Kaydee were going to go back to Mikey's parent's house that night because Mikey had an early-morning mandatory baseball workout.

I said my good nights and went to bed.

In the middle of the night, Allee came into our room. I remember looking up and seeing her silhouette at the door, the light from the hallway shining behind her. She said, "Someone's at the door; I think it's Mikey and Kaydee."

Craig jumped up, and I got out of bed, thinking, "Why would Mikey and Kaydee have come back home?" I went to my bedroom door and from there I could look over the upstairs railing down to the front door. I gasped when I saw the fire chief standing at our front door in his freshly starched uniform.

I turned back into my bedroom to get my robe and remember uttering under my breath, "No, no, no, no!" I was only halfway down the stairs when I saw Craig take a step back from the open front door, holding his chest. And then came the words out of Craig's mouth, "Is Mikey still alive?"

At that moment, my world stopped.

My body and mind went numb. My ears stopped hearing, and my mind stopped thinking. I felt hot, then cold, and then nothing. My body sat down on the stairs and was disconnected from my thoughts. I had made it only halfway down the staircase. My arms clutched the banister, and then I heard myself scream.

When my mouth stopped screaming, I heard a voice behind me. As clear as day, I heard the voice say, "I took the right one." I turned to see who would say such a thing at that moment, but there was no one there.

I later learned to whom that voice belongs, because I've heard it many times since then. It was the Holy Spirit. When the Spirit speaks, He speaks to the point.

Analyzing our family and Kaydee's role in the family, He was right. Being the amazing person she was, it was Kaydee's life that would impact the most people. The story of her life would do the most for the greater good. Her smile was the one that would light up any room. Her gift of listening was the one that everyone wished to possess. Her friendship was the one that everyone longed for. Her beauty was beyond external: she was internally radiant. Her humor was what good times were made of. Her eyes were so blue and angelic, you could sink into them. Her soul personified authenticity. Yes, Kaydee had "it." I believe her light shined so brightly that people were just drawn to it as if her spirit were addictive.

Remembering specific details about that night is difficult, and what felt like a minute could have been an hour. Hazy memories of that night include Craig's best friend, Steve, holding out his hand to take mine so we could move into the family room, where the fire department pastor could explain to us what had happened. Walking into the family room and sitting down on the couch, my mind was spinning with many thoughts, but I was unable to express a rational one. There were no tears at first. I wasn't crying. I couldn't. I just couldn't. The news was so crushing to my soul that my body took over and pumped just enough oxygen to my heart and brain to survive. The rest shut down in shock.

I couldn't think. I couldn't speak. I could hardly breathe. I didn't want to breathe. I wanted to die with Kaydee. I remember asking God to take me Home because I just wanted to be with my Kaydee. Tears wouldn't come, but my face felt numb and seemed to be puffing up. It felt like the tears were trapped behind my skin and my face was filling up with sorrow.

The fire chief spoke first and explained that Kaydee and Mikey had come upon an accident on the freeway. They had stopped because a young girl who was involved in the accident had gotten out of her car and was wandering dangerously out into traffic. Kaydee had gotten out of the car with Mikey to give first aid to the girl, who was bleeding from a head wound. Kaydee instructed Mikey to get a towel from the trunk of his car, and when he did, a drunk driver came crashing through the accident scene and hit the back of Mikey's car. Mikey's life was spared when he jumped out of the way of the speeding car. Witnesses say that Kaydee threw herself over the girl to protect her from the impact. The young girl survived, but Kaydee died instantly.

Mikey would later tell me that he ran to Kaydee after the car struck her and saw her lying on her side on the pavement. He described her face at that moment as pink and radiant. All he could think to do was drop to his knees in prayer.

How beautiful that God would allow him to see Kaydee in His glory and that Mikey would have that image to remember so that the horrific sounds and sights of the accident might be blurred in his memory.

Our son, Cody, was having a very difficult time with the horrifying news and was trying not to hyperventilate, interlocking his fingers behind his head, with his elbows out to the side and pacing around the kitchen. He grabbed a Bible and began reciting Scripture.

Craig vowed out loud to all of us that this tragedy would not tear our family apart, but that we would be closer than ever. Allee went outside with her boyfriend and walked up and down the street in the rain for hours. Taylor just lay with her head in my lap.

It wasn't until other family members arrived that I began to cry. When I saw the look on their faces, reality set in, and I realized how much pain this tragedy was going to cause our entire family. I needed God to tell me that we would be okay. And with tender mercy, He began showing us signs of His amazing grace.

Over the next few days almost everyone we've ever known visited or called us, offering their love and prayers. It was overwhelming. Every time we turned around, another bouquet of sympathy made its way into our home.

Along with these visits of love from our family and friends came little love notes from our sweet Lord: mysterious events that we couldn't explain but that gave us comfort. These were the first of many more "God winks" that we have since experienced. It was as if He needed to show us how He would communicate with us, so that later, when we needed to hear it, we could understand His love language.

The very first one happened the day after the accident. Passing by Kaydee's bedroom, I saw her open suitcase. I began to take the clothes out and hold them close to me. I inhaled long and hard to smell the perfume left on her clothing. Taking out the sweater that she had worn the day before for our Christmas pictures, I held it close to my face. There was a mirror on the wall in front of me and I caught a glimpse of the back of the sweater in the reflection. I turned the sweater around to take a closer look and realized that there were angel wings on the back of it. The sweater she wore the day she went to heaven was adorned with lovely angel wings, and I wore that same sweater to her Rosary. It was a blessing from God to be able to have her spirit wrapped around me for comfort that night.

The God winks continued over the next few days and, by His mercy, continue to this day. It's difficult to explain how it feels when they happen; we are all naturally doubting Thomases. The initial reaction is always the same: "No, it can't be." Or, "Wow, that's weird." After a while, though, we began to recognize that they were simply God's way of saying, "I am with you." It seemed that the more we surrendered to God's will, the more He spoke directly to us in ways that were definitely not of this world.

People often ask us how we didn't lose our faith after this tragedy. To this day, I can't answer that question succinctly, except to say that through His grace, we realized early on that God had called us by name for this journey. He sent us constant messages through others, such as these words of St. Justin Martyr, which became our mantra: "The greatest grace God can give someone is to send him a trial he cannot bear with his own powers — and then sustain him with His grace so he may endure to the end and be saved."[2] God saw us relying on our Catholic Faith and coming to the grace-filled sacraments often. I believe that in His mercy, he sent us these little God winks so that the cross He had asked us to carry might feel a little lighter.

I have always been a numbers person. My husband relies on me for phone numbers, account numbers, social security numbers,

---

[2] From the Litany of the Counsel of the Saints.

and addresses, and God has used numbers over and over again to reveal Himself to me in the most amazing ways.

In our house when the kids were growing up, we taught them that if they saw 11:11 on a clock, it meant angels were talking to them; and then the kids would make a wish. A few days after the accident, Allee found on Facebook a message that Kaydee had sent to her while she was away at college. It was a picture of an alarm clock that read 11:11. The caption read, "I'm wishing for you."

Every year we take a family trip back to the University of Notre Dame to watch Irish football. Our last family vacation with Kaydee was to Notre Dame just a few months before her death. After Kaydee was gone, and knowing she would have wanted us to, we decided to keep with our tradition and attend our annual football game. As we drove from the airport to our usual hotel at Notre Dame, memories of Kaydee pierced our hearts.

When we got to the hotel, Craig dropped us off in front, and we went to check in while he parked the car. It was surreal being back at the same hotel where we had been with Kaydee. So many memories and feelings came flooding back. I was beating myself up for not choosing a different hotel when the man behind the desk handed me our room keys. He said, "Here you go, Mrs. Campbell. You're in room 1111." In an instant, my heart pain was gone. I had to laugh when I saw Craig's face at the door of room 1111. Such moments bring us together as husband and wife, forever connected by the gravity of a loss only the two of us can understand.

The day of the Rosary was difficult. We decided to keep the casket closed because we never saw Kaydee after the accident and had agreed that we would prefer to remember her as she looked the night she left our house. Earlier that day, one of the firefighters had handed me a bag from the coroner's office that contained Kaydee's personal items. An overwhelming emptiness enveloped me.

Opening it and reaching in, I took out her wallet, her earrings, and a rosary. Scanning the coroner's report inside the bag, I came to a checked box that said she was wearing a "beaded necklace." My daughter never wore a rosary—ever. But on the day of her death and resurrection into Heaven, she decided to wear one; and I received it on the day of her Rosary.

Shortly after her death and after much prayer and discernment, I consecrated myself to our Blessed Mother and now say a Rosary every day. It's truly a weapon against despair and brings a peace that is beyond human understanding. I still have that rosary hanging on my bedpost, where it will stay forever.

The day of the funeral was tough. Getting ready, I remember watching my hands shake and begging for God's mercy to help us survive it. After I asked God for assistance, He turned my feelings of fear into feelings of celebration of Kaydee's new life in Heaven. He showed me that death simply means a new life for our loved ones who have completed their journey here and passed through this life into the next—a new life with no suffering, only complete peace and joy.

By allowing us to experience His sweetness through God winks, God taught us that eternal life is real. The teachings of the Catholic Church about eternal life became a true source of joy in the midst of our suffering.

After my change of heart about the funeral, an unexpected acceptance set in. Our Lord instilled in all of us a comforting wisdom. We saw that there was no way around this day and that we just had to plow through it with grace. In His wisdom, on numerous occasions that day, the same Scripture passage — Isaiah 41:10 — was sent to us by different people: "Do not fear: I am with you; do not be anxious: I am your God. I will strengthen you; I will help you; I will uphold you with my victorious right hand."

And He did.

On the day of the funeral, more than fifteen hundred people gathered to pay their respects to Kaydee. As we were exiting the church, the entire Fire Department Pipes and Drums Band played "Amazing Grace." As Kaydee's casket was carried in front of us, my husband saw a white butterfly flying around it. We were all very emotional during the song, and when we got into the limousine afterward, we were somber and quiet. My husband asked, "Did you see that butterfly flying around the casket?" We immediately asked what color it was. My husband said, "White, why?"

In high school, Kaydee had gone on a retreat and told me a story when she got home. She said she was meditating and was thinking about her deceased great aunt, JinJin. We had been blessed to be able to take JinJin into our home when she became terminally ill so that she didn't have to pass away in a hospital or a nursing home.

JinJin was the most devout Catholic I have ever known before or since, and it was a beautiful and faith-filled experience for my kids to be able to listen to her talk about her excitement about Heaven.

JinJin was about four feet six inches tall and would always tell everyone that she was going to be six feet tall in Heaven and be a ballerina with long legs.

Kaydee explained that she was thinking about how JinJin used to say this and at that very moment, a white butterfly started to "dance" around her. To honor JinJin's memory, Kaydee decided to tattoo a little white butterfly on her wrist.

Because Kaydee had already been what we considered "silly enough" to get a previous tattoo, we didn't tell her dad about this one since he wasn't too happy about the other one. Since it was white, you could hardly see it anyway, so we thought that was information that maybe we should just keep quiet.

So what we all knew, and what my husband didn't know, was that Kaydee had a little outline of a white butterfly tattooed on her wrist. Remember, the day of the funeral was in the middle of winter, the mountains are covered with snow and a little white butterfly appears? Miracles do happen. How clever of God to reveal the white butterfly to the only person who didn't know about her tattoo.

Toby Keith had been Kaydee's favorite country music star. Allee went to a Toby Keith concert with her friends, and there she met the love of her life, Mike. His middle name is Anthony. Kaydee's boyfriend, Mikey, also has the middle name of Anthony. So when Allee found out that their boyfriends shared the same first and middle names, she wondered if her Mike might be "the one."

In fact, he did turn out to be the one and when, a few years after Kaydee's death, they bought their first home, Allee discovered that the previous owners had left something in the garden: a beautiful white butterfly garden stone, God's way of allowing our Kaydee to send a message of congratulations and love to her sister.

When Taylor found her soul mate, we had a feeling Kaydee had her hand in it somehow. Kaydee loved to hear Taylor sing and would put in her song requests often. When Taylor met Shane, I knew immediately that he had been found especially for Taylor. Shane was one of Craig's reserve firefighters and was at our home after the funeral with many others showing support. The kids found comfort singing worship songs, and Shane tells us that when he heard Taylor's voice, he thought she sounded like an angel and fell in love.

Last year, Taylor and Shane were fortunate enough to buy their first home. The previous owner took everything when she left except for one thing—a huge white butterfly yard ornament hanging on the back fence.

These are only two instances of white-butterfly God winks and there have been more than we can count, but I will share the most memorable of all. One day, Allee and I visited Kaydee's grave at the cemetery. As Allee was standing above Kaydee's grave marker, she whipped her head backward and cried, "Mom! Did you see that butterfly? It just did a fly-by right past my face!" She started to laugh, and it wasn't a few seconds before another butterfly did the same thing. She screamed with delight, and within a minute we were surrounded by hundreds of butterflies. We looked up, and they were all over the cemetery.

How on earth do you explain that?

Cody spent years preparing for a career as a firefighter and he was lucky enough to get picked in a lottery to test for one of the largest fire departments in California. Since this was a huge opportunity, he was very nervous, but God knew he needed peace and was about to give him a huge dose of it.

Cody stopped for coffee on the way to the test, and his change happened to be $11.11. When he got to the test, he parked his car in front of a dirt hill and noticed that someone had etched a large cross in the dirt. With a little more confidence after these two God winks, he joined up with some friends who had gathered in front of the building for the test.

A young man walked up to the circle of men and Cody asked him what time it was. The young man looked at his watch and said, "It's 11:11." He then held out his hand to introduce himself. He said, "Hi, I'm Angel." Cody made Angel call me because he didn't think I would believe it. He passed that test and went on to become a firefighter for that department, where he has worked for several years now.

Throughout our grief journey, we were given so many of these tender consolations from our Lord. What surprised us about His mercies during suffering is how they helped connect our head knowledge to our heartstrings. We always believed in eternal life, but now we are blessed to *know* there is eternal life. We never could have anticipated the many ways that God was able to teach us and convince us of our Catholic Faith and His love for us through permitting our precious daughter to be taken from us in this earthly life.

The Catholic Church's teachings on the virtues of hope and faith and joy helped us avoid the rocks of despair. Our Lord brought great Catholic people into our lives to help guide us through our grief. Eucharistic Adoration was introduced to us and proved to be tremendously therapeutic for our souls. My husband has an extremely short attention span and admits that he cannot stay in one place very long without getting antsy. Somehow, though, when we go to Eucharistic Adoration he's able to sit quietly in prayer for an hour or more. The grace we receive from Adoration is like a salve we use to heal our wounded hearts.

We learned early on that Satan is ready to pounce at our most vulnerable times. We learned to shake him off by praying unceasingly and using the sacraments and devotions to ward off his attempts to cause us to despair. Our Catholic Faith carried us through. We went to Eucharistic Adoration often and with an openness to grace that we had never had before.

We were beggars for mercy at the table of our Lord, and He answered our pleas with love, comfort, and peace. The sacraments of Confession and the Holy Eucharist sustained us and enabled us to shoulder the crushing weight of our suffering and grief over losing Kaydee. The very life of Jesus Himself, His sanctifying grace in the sacraments of the Catholic Church, surprised us with its power and healing comfort. It is literally true that we were "surprised by life" each time we encountered Jesus in the sacraments and He helped us carry our cross.

We also learned profound lessons about *suffering*. No one wants to suffer; and yet, when we offer our suffering to the Lord, He lifts us above worldly distractions and temptations, causing us to look deep into our own souls for the answers He offers.

Before Kaydee's death, we could have easily become a Catholic family that slipped into secularism and materialism, but for a long time after Kaydee's death, I was completely oblivious to the popular movies, television shows, social trends, and other worldly fads that many others were focused on. I could not have cared less about any of it. God had changed my focus, redirecting my gaze to what is most important: eternal life.

He continued teaching me a huge life lesson about how all the Catholic Church's teachings on life issues (marriage, contraception, abortion, euthanasia) really make complete sense and have their most profound meaning only *in light of* the main life issue: His promise of eternal life to those who love Him and who willingly take up their cross and follow Him. As I began to understand this truth in greater simplicity, the Catholic Church's teachings on life issues became clearer, more meaningful, and a joy to accept and embrace.

As I reflect on how our Catholic Faith has grown since Kaydee's death, I realize how profoundly aware I now am that suffering is necessary. The Church's teaching on the Communion of Saints has been a major help to me as I've journeyed through grief and acceptance, as I've befriended many of the saints in heaven, and as I still ask for their intercession almost daily, having learned how much they all suffered lovingly for Jesus. Now I understand why.

I don't mean that suffering has been or should be easy, because it can truly be terrifying at times. But I've learned that when we offer our suffering to the Lord, it ignites a fire in the soul that can burn so intensely that it feels at times as if we are dying of love from the inside out. I discovered that some of the great saints, such as St. Teresa of Avila, described this burning fire of God's love similarly. I found that when the "old you" has been burned away, the real and authentic you begins to emerge. Suffering, when offered to God, leads us to Him.

I wish to hear only one thing when I meet God face-to-face: "Well done, good and faithful servant. Welcome Home."

DOREEN CAMPBELL is a cradle Catholic, and her husband, Craig, is a twenty-year convert to the Faith. Doreen has been a registered nurse for more than thirty years, and Craig is a retired fire captain and paramedic who spent his career caring for the sick and the dying. Doreen is an Extraordinary Minister of the Eucharist for the homebound and a prayer warrior on the San Francisco Solano prayer team. Doreen and Craig enjoy spending time with their three grandchildren, the joy in their lives, and hope to be blessed with many more. The Campbells live in Southern California.

CDCKTA@ATT.NET

GOODBYE, CONTRACEPTION; HELLO, NFP!

SHAUN AND JESSICA MCAFEE

From Shaun:

Long before we trusted the Catholic Church or even considered marriage, my wife and I got into a heated debate about abortion.

"So you think abortion is a sin?"

"There's no question: it's wrong," she said, as if it should have been obvious.

"What gives you the right to say that? I think there are several cases where a mother should have the choice to have an abortion."

"Like what?" she replied.

"Well, what happens if a father rapes his daughter?"

"Um ..."

"And what about the mother who is addicted to drugs?"

"Well …"

"See what I mean now?"

"No. Absolutely not! There's no case in which a woman should abort her child. You gave two examples in which you think it would be good for that child based on outcomes you can't predict. Do you just end lives because you *think* a life might be of less quality? I think all lives have limitless quality!"

"Um …"

She was making a good point. She continued:

"Then there's the fact that you're punishing an unborn child for the mistakes of adults."

"But why would you force a child to be born with a disability?"

"Why would you take life away from any child? You're not even giving them a chance! Some of the happiest people I've known are kids with Down syndrome, and their parents are filled with love for their kid."

"…"

"Well?"

"Well, I just think women should have a choice. I guess I would put it this way: personally, I'm pro-life; I would never have or encourage an abortion. But at the same time, I think, legally, women should have a choice. I mean, how can we take away someone's free will?"

We didn't talk more about abortion that day or for many months to come. Talking about pro-life issues can be incredibly frustrating for disagreeing parties. Her opinion made some sense at the time, but it didn't persuade me to abandon my sentiments on the subject. Even though we disagreed, what Jessica told me that day has come to mind every time I've had a conversation about pro-life issues.

GOODBYE, CONTRACEPTION; HELLO, NFP!

From Jessica:

I remember the conversation Shaun mentions. His tone shocked me, and, like him, I've not forgotten it.

I went silent. That's when I first realized we were not on the same page on the pro-life issue. He agreed that an abortion shouldn't happen just because a baby was inconvenient. However, Shaun said, "It wasn't that simple in real life." He told me he had once helped a woman consider whether to abort her baby. The father wasn't someone she was with any longer. She felt trapped between two bad alternatives: being tied to a man she didn't want to be with, or being a young single mother. Months later, Shawn looked up the woman on Facebook and was surprised by her profile picture with a beautiful baby girl. Shaun was immediately taken with the baby.

"Are you happy she didn't abort the baby?"

"Jess..."

"Think about it. Had she made that decision, regardless of when you think life begins, that little girl would not be alive. Period."

The conversation went on to the usual: rape, incest, birth defects, and handicaps. I had the classic, thought-provoking answers. In the end, he left the conversation saying he thought women should have the choice, and I left it saying that everything possible should be done to save and bring dignity to both lives—mother and baby, but especially the innocent baby.

When we realized our relationship was heading toward marriage, I brought the subject up again. Abortion was a deal breaker for me. Although Shaun's beliefs weren't as strong as mine, I was relieved that in the meantime he had become very pro-baby as well as pro-woman.

From Shaun:

Fast forward a year: we were planning to be married; there was lots to discuss, and we wanted to be responsible. Our plan was, after about a year of being married, for me to get out of the military so I could finish my undergraduate degree.

We agreed that having a child was something we wanted, but not immediately, and so I asked Jessica if she would go on birth control. Jessica hesitated for health reasons, so I said I would go to the doctor with her. The doctor assuaged all of her concerns. From there, it seemed as easy as choosing a method. Was she going to take a shot? Pop pills? Wear a patch?

For reasons I don't remember, Jessica decided to receive her birth control with the shot. One shot provided birth control for about ninety days, which eliminated problems that would arise if she forgot to take a pill.

For me, the goal was to make the issue "out of sight, out of mind." To achieve my educational goals and maintain the integrity of my future family, using birth control was a no-brainer. I convinced myself that postponing children now would be better for kids born later.

It was 2008, and the job market was weak. With my unemployment imminent, I didn't want to start our new life together without a solid plan. Since money problems were a major cause of divorce, I was convinced that the thirty-dollar cost of birth control was better for our marriage than the thousands of dollars it costs to have children — at least until I got my college degree and had a good job.

From Jessica:

Shaun and I had a very short engagement — just under a month! He had been working very hard on his degree and had to complete it. My dream was to be a stay-at-home mom. We needed to work as a team on a strict plan. Time wasn't on our side because of reproductive problems I had, so we wanted to work fast to get to a place where we could have babies.

We decided to postpone children for at least the first two years of our marriage and then revisit the topic. That meant we needed to choose a responsible method of family planning. We wanted to ensure the egg and the sperm would never meet, but if they somehow did, that life wouldn't be aborted by the contraceptive. We wouldn't risk the life of our baby, planned or not.

The doctor allayed all our worries. He assured us that we could use any of the following methods without compromising our will to protect life at every stage from conception onward: the implant, the shot, the pill, or the patch.

We chose the shot, the easiest of the methods. The nurse administered it while Shaun held my hand, and within ten minutes I felt nauseated and lightheaded. I was glad Shaun was there to drive us home. I hoped that the symptoms were the result of stress. On the way home Shaun thanked me, saying he wished there was a way he could take the shot instead of its being a burden laid solely on my shoulders.

From Shaun:

Before we were married we had what was for us responsible discussions about the future of our family. How many kids we should have? How should we space them? Did we want boys or girls?

I didn't realize it at the time, but these questions were selfish. I see now that they weren't really "responsible" conversations. We were concerned with convenience and selection, as if having a family works well only when it is arranged around material or professional goals. Unconsciously, we had judged that we could not take part in the creative act of childbearing unless we determined how, when, and where it happened. As good as our intentions were — not to form a family that we couldn't manage — we were deeply mistaken about our obligations in marriage.

After two years of preventing pregnancy through contraception, I earned my undergraduate degree and landed a decent job. One night in September, Jessica was brushing her teeth, and I said to her, "Jessica, I'm ready to have kids. Can you stop taking birth control?"

I've only seen her that happy a few times. It's a unique sort of satisfaction that filled her face. It was a mix of "Really? Are you sure?" and "*Definitely!*"

We stopped the contraception immediately, hoping she would be pregnant soon. But we had a tough road ahead of us.

From Jessica:

The shot was horrible. Horrible!

I woke up every morning so nauseated I couldn't function for the first half hour, was miserable until noon, and miserable again at bedtime. I had daily headaches, was always tired, constantly "spotting," and emotional. I had to force myself to eat well when I didn't want to eat at all, and I gained weight at an alarming pace. I had had two rounds of the shot when, in a social situation, I met the nurse who had administered the shot to me.

She told me about methods of contraception she couldn't believe were legal, and what women complained about. The thing that she said she hated most in her job was giving women that shot and not being allowed to warn them ahead of time what they were in for, knowing two of the doctors gave poor information.

I requested a different doctor.

I would love to say that this is when I wised up and did my own research and at minimum read the small print for each of the methods we considered, but I did not. I have no one to blame except myself.

Next I tried the patch, which became increasingly unpleasant. I was glad when we ran out. Shaun was no longer in the military, and we had no health insurance. Although we both worked long hours, we had minimal income.

Someone recommended that I get the pill from Planned Parenthood.

Wasn't that the place that does abortions? I wasn't sure, but if it was, I wanted no part of it.

So I called.

The receptionist said they didn't perform abortions, so I made an appointment. One small step at a time, our use of contraception — even while we tried to protect life — led me to the doors of Planned Parenthood.

The waiting room was well lit and comfortable. I couldn't find anything about abortions anywhere. I was looking for any reason to bolt. Sexually transmitted diseases and safe sex seemed to be the push. I went back to the room with the provider, who gave me my annual physical and a prescription for three months of the pill — the most affordable method they provided. She seemed as if she truly cared about me. She told me, when I asked, that their clinic did not perform abortions, but others did.

As I checked out, they pushed for full payment, which I didn't have. Eventually the receptionist said they would cover half. I didn't want to give them my business, but if I did, at least they were footing part of the bill.

The next two years I bit my tongue a lot and wondered when, if ever, we would try for babies. Then it finally happened.

Shaun came home from work one day thoughtful and quiet. That evening, he said, "Jess, I think I'm ready for us to have a baby. If we keep waiting for the perfect situation, it may never come. But we can make it work. What do you think about coming off the pill?"

Only a few times in my life have I been that happy and excited. I couldn't hug him tight enough. I flushed the rest of the pills the same hour. A week later I couldn't believe how good I felt; it was like someone had physically lifted a weight off my body and a fog had cleared. I told Shaun I didn't care what we had to do in the future, I wouldn't be going back on contraception. He laughed, thinking I was just happy we were trying to conceive. But two weeks passed, and he noticed the differences in me as well.

From Shaun:

Days after I asked her at the bathroom sink if it would be alright to stop using birth control, I remember inquiring with excitement, "So have you stopped taking the pill?" She assured me she had. "Great!" I remember thinking. "You'll be pregnant soon."

But those couple of days turned into a couple of months, and still no sign of pregnancy. I asked her about it—why it might be taking a while—and she told me that it would take time for the hormones completely to exit her system.

I had to be patient.

Around nine months went by.

"How long should this take?"

As much as I tried not to stress about it, I was worried that our use of contraception had left Jessica sterile. I was afraid to ask her the questions that haunted me: "What have I done? Is my wife barren now?"

GOODBYE, CONTRACEPTION; HELLO, NFP!

From Jessica:

The likelihood of infertility and miscarriage tormented me. I placed my desire for children in God's hands and continually had to remind myself to trust God. He could make fertile even a barren womb. He alone could bring forth a life—no one else could.

I had cried and prayed over so many of my friends and heard of their infertility struggles, the doctors, the injections, and the humiliating intrusion into the most intimate areas, with sex becoming a chore and their hearts sinking at every negative pregnancy test, month after month. Worst were the miscarriages.

Rather than worry, I made a plan. We would give it a year of trying, and I wouldn't get my hopes up in that time. I plugged everything into an app, and we focused in on days it said we were fertile.

Shaun was due to go on a business trip over the time our app said I was next going to ovulate, so we set ourselves up to let it go for a month and a half. While he was gone, I had a lot of time to myself to think things through. I finally let myself feel it all: the fear, the disappointment, the hope I didn't even realize had been building. I steeled myself for what would likely be a long road toward getting the family we wanted through fertility treatments or adoption, or both. I didn't know how we would afford either, but we would figure it out.

I pulled myself together and was refreshed with a newfound trust that God's plan was greater than mine: He would lead and provide for each step, and He would use the pain and disappointment for good somehow. I again handed Him my hopes and begged Him to return them in one way or another.

Shaun came home, and just over a week later I took my habitual pregnancy test before having a glass of wine.

It was positive!

My heart soared!

I couldn't wait to tell Shaun we were going to be parents!

From Shaun:

While we were trying to conceive, I began considering the Catholic Church. For me, authority, morals, and sexuality were big stumbling blocks. "How could a group of people be free from doctrinal and moral error?" The way I saw it, nobody could be free from error except for Christ Himself, and claiming to "know it all" smacked of blasphemy, equating a creature with the Creator.

As I began reading Catholic books, however, I often found myself thinking, "Well, that actually makes a lot of sense. I'd better keep reading to see where this argument falls apart." Next thing you know, I'd be at the end of the book. "Better get out another book, because Catholic morality can't be flawless."

Next book, same result: arguments that were complete, charitable, and satisfying. Not only did they thoroughly explain the Catholic Church's position and the defense thereof; they revealed the terrible errors in my own logic, much of which was made up of what I had learned as a Protestant.

One thing helped me immensely as I drew closer to the Church: an understanding of her authority. Once I came to see that it came not from the Bible, but directly from Jesus by way of the apostles (who later wrote much of the New Testament), almost all of my issues with Catholic teachings evaporated.

Two of the Church's moral stances continued to trouble me, however: her prohibition of abortion and of artificial contraception. I wanted to confess my sins of supporting pro-choice ideologies and using birth control, but I still did not understand *why* they were judged to be sinful.

GOODBYE, CONTRACEPTION; HELLO, NFP!

I suffered from a classic case of relativism, a powerful, seductive, and deceptive heresy that denies all universal truths, holding that their truth or falsehood depends on how they are judged by any individual.

I had always been personally against abortion but thought that it should be a personal decision for a woman. I thought that if a woman truly believed abortion was right, then it was, in fact, right for her. Clearly, I was confused about the application of universal moral truths.

The answer to one question destroyed my relativism: "If the unborn child is truly a child, then how can killing him be wrong for me but licit for someone else?"

Overcoming my relativism brought healing, consolation, and reconciliation. Next, I had to decide how I would treat birth control.

Frankly, I had never given birth control much thought. The word *contraception* seemed more medical than anything else. Since my teen years I had heard stories from female friends about how their parents had them on birth control. These parents claimed that it was not that their teen was sexually active; rather, they said, the pill provided regularity in their menstrual cycle. So, from the onset, it seemed perfectly responsible to use birth control.

Any conversation I had with my wife or Christian friends about birth control mainly addressed the physical risks, rather than the moral questions. In the decades I had been an Evangelical, I never once heard a sermon about birth control. Not once.

Interestingly, this was one of the first things I learned about the Catholic Church; but I wasn't impressed when I learned that many Catholics ignore the Church's prohibition of artificial contraception. So if I was going to become an obedient Catholic, which I wanted very much, I had to understand the immorality of contraception prior to making my first confession.

Although I didn't realize it at first, my former opinion on abortion was related to my opinion on birth control. It seemed evident to me that birth control would reduce unwanted pregnancies and therefore would reduce abortions. So birth control seemed to be a force for good. I assumed that people on birth control were no more or less prone to promiscuity than those who didn't use it. In fact, in repeated studies, birth control has been directly shown to promote sex outside marriage and with multiple partners. It has aided in the creation of a society that values the pleasures of sex over sexual responsibility.

I was wrong about artificial birth control as a positive force in society, but I still needed the Christian basis for saying it is immoral. Where was I to look? Naturally, I searched the Bible but nothing there directly referred to contraception.

Or did it?

Online, I came across a reference to the story of Onan. I thought to myself, "I know this story, but it has nothing to do with birth control. It's about masturbation."

But what did masturbation have to do with birth control? *Everything.*

Since Onan spilled his "seed" (semen) to avoid procreation, God's condemnation of Onan shows His disapproval of sexual acts that are not open to life. When couples use withdrawal to avoid pregnancy, it is mutual masturbation. Absolutely preventing conception in this way—or any other way—is contrary to God's law. Couples who use devices, techniques, or hormones to prevent conception violate the very nature of the act of intercourse.

I realized that my sins were equal to Onan's, and I was in desperate need of God's grace and forgiveness. To my relief, I was soon to become Catholic and could enter the Church with a clean conscience after my first confession.

In a matter of months, through my uncompromising search for the truth and my desire to follow Christ, I had gone from a pro-choice, birth control–endorsing relativist to a Christian in full communion with the social and moral teaching of the Catholic Church. I made my first confession on Good Friday 2012, and the next day I receive my first Eucharist and was confirmed.

From Jessica:

After telling Shaun I was pregnant, I set about to find doctors who would do everything in their power to protect our unborn baby in the womb. That led me to NaProTECHNOLOGY, which specializes in women's reproductive care, especially in infertility and bringing high-risk pregnancies to term.

The NaPro medical staff treated me with a courtesy I had never experienced before and extended it to Shaun and to our baby as well. From the start, I was in their office every two weeks receiving the care I needed to maintain a healthy pregnancy.

After the baby was born, we began charting my cycles using the Creighton Model method. The longer we charted, the more trust I had in it. Not only did it teach us to manage our fertility, but we were encouraged to be mindful of all the various aspects of our relationship. As we learned to trust each other with our fertility, our trust in each other in general grew. I can honestly say that managing our fertility and seeing the dignity it brought to my marriage and my family drew me to the Catholic Church. When we were expecting our second baby, our FertilityCare office approached me, offering me a scholarship to become a practitioner myself.

Charting was much more than a different form of contraception. I learned the actual effects of artificial contraception on women, on marriages, and on the culture as a whole. I learned that the pill is a class-one carcinogen, and that it also weakens the lining of the uterus to cause early miscarriage in cases where conception manages to occur. Moreover, some forms of artificial birth control also disguise the symptoms of curable diseases, causing women not to get the treatment they need.

During my training, I fell in love with *Humanae Vitae*, the celebrated encyclical of Pope Paul VI. It explains God's design for marriage and love, and presents responsible parenthood as a vocation we should take seriously and manage as good stewards. It promotes the dignity of all human life in a straightforward, no-nonsense way.

"Value of Self-Discipline" is one of my favorite paragraphs in *Humanae Vitae*. In it, periodic abstinence is not presented as easy. Instead, the encyclical encourages us to see the positive effects of periodic abstinence. Practicing self-control helps us to value ourselves and each other. A further benefit is the value children feel from growing up in a loving marriage that holds strongly to these truths. Says *Humanae Vitae*:

> [Periodic abstinence] brings to family life abundant fruits of tranquillity and peace. It helps in solving difficulties of other kinds. It fosters in husband and wife thoughtfulness and loving consideration for one another. It helps them to repel inordinate self-love, which is the opposite of charity. It arouses in them a consciousness of their responsibilities. And finally, it confers upon parents a deeper and more effective influence in the education of their children. As their children grow up, they develop a right sense of values and achieve a serene and harmonious use of their mental and physical powers. (no. 21)

This moral training was providential to me because, until then, I had a very contraceptive mind-set regarding natural family planning. Although I liked NFP better than the pill because I wasn't altering my body, I didn't see the fundamental difference between the pill and NFP. I had to ask myself, "Why is artificial contraception a sin, but NFP is not?"

Pope John Paul II and Pope Paul VI acknowledge that there are many pleasures in sex but remind us that it has only two fundamental purposes: unity and procreation. Obviously, sex is how babies are made, but our society sees babies as a risk of sex rather than the blessed fruit of sexual union.

When we don't accept both purposes of sex, we rob ourselves and our spouse of its wholeness, its life-giving power, and its total unity. In fact, we rob our spouse of his inherent human dignity by saying, "I like everything about you—except the way your body is inconveniently fertile."

In his encyclical *Familiaris Consortio*, John Paul II puts this well:

> When couples, by means of recourse to contraception, separate these two meanings that God the Creator has inscribed in the being of man and woman and in the dynamism of their sexual communion, they act as "arbiters" of the divine plan and they "manipulate" and degrade human sexuality—and with it themselves and their married partner—by altering its value of "total" self-giving.... When, instead, by means of recourse to periods of infertility, the couple respect the inseparable connection between the unitive and procreative meanings of human sexuality, they are acting as "ministers" of God's plan and they "benefit from" their sexuality

according to the original dynamism of "total" self-giving, without manipulation or alteration. (no. 32)

Sexuality is a gift we give and receive in totality, holding nothing back, never using one another as a means to an end, but always going back to the two purposes of this sexual aspect of our relationship. When Shaun and I began charting, I managed our fertility as a burden instead of the powerful gift it is. I robbed my marriage during that time. In a letter to the director of the Centre for Research and Study on the Natural Regulation of Fertility, John Paul II writes:

> In the act that expresses their love, spouses are called to make a reciprocal gift of themselves to each other in the totality of their person: nothing that is part of their being can be excluded from this gift.

Denying oneself isn't always pleasant, but when done for the correct reasons, a husband and wife say to each other, "I cherish you, everything about you, so much that I would deny myself on occasion rather than alter you in any way."

Contraception and natural family planning are worlds apart, and I'm grateful to have come to understand this in my Faith and within my marriage. Since we began practicing self-control together, stopped holding back parts of our personhood from one another, and worked responsibly as a team without denying God's ultimate control, the peace and unity we have achieved is unlike anything we experienced before. We have become more giving, more loving, more accepting, and we aren't afraid of our own fertility or of a method "failing" us.

Today, Shaun and I have been blessed with three wonderful children who are among the greatest sources of joy in our lives:

Gabriel, Tristan, and Dominic. We have healed from the negative effects of contraception in our marriage and are thrilled to encourage others to discover the same freedom found in practicing true, authentic love with the use of natural family planning.

SHAUN AND JESSICA MCAFEE were married in 2008 and entered the Catholic Church four years later. Jessica is happily busy as a stay-at-home mother, while Shaun works for the Army Corps of Engineers and writes for the *National Catholic Register* and for *Catholic Answers Magazine* Online, of which he is also the editor. They are from Omaha, Nebraska, but currently live in Japan.

SHAUNMCO4@GMAIL.COM

TWITTER @SHAUNMCAFEE

BYE, BYE, BOYS AND BOOZE

SHALIMAR MASTERS

The streetlights dimly lit the night through the chilling drizzle, but I ignored the cold and my determination to get to Mass. I was less than a block from my parents' home, yet I called them from a pay phone, common fixtures throughout the countryside of that small town not far from Oxford, England, in the mid-1990s, just before modern cell phones became commonplace. I needed my parents to give me a ride to Sunday evening Mass if I was to make it on time, as I did not have a driver's license.

Just nineteen, I had been out partying and clubbing the night before, was hung over most of Sunday, and had not made it to Mass that morning with the rest of my family, with whom I lived. Although I had been a party girl since I was sixteen, I somehow clung to the Faith in which I was raised, as imperfectly as I lived it. Sunday Mass was simply not to be skipped; by my devout parents, I had been taught — and believed — that it was a mortal sin to do so.

Nevertheless, to my surprise and despite my pleading, the voice on the other end of the damp pay phone said, "No."

I hadn't followed the rules; I hadn't checked all the right boxes; it was inconvenient for them, and I had apparently missed my chance. I was told not to call their Catholic friends for a ride either. Although heartbreaking, that rejection by my family was not nearly as frightful as my fear of God for missing Mass through my own fault. So I called my atheist boyfriend's parents.

They said yes.

Of all people, they drove me to Mass that evening. To them, it was no big deal; it was kids being kids. They rushed over, dropped me off at evening Mass, waited for me outside, and welcomed me back to their fancy home for dinner.

This one event changed my whole outlook, my behavior, and my faith for the next two and a half years: that Sunday night, I turned away from my family and away from the Faith.

As a child, I had deep and unsatisfied longings. I remember my Grampie as a quiet, holy man, tall and strong. When I fell at the playground and cut open my chin, he scooped me up in his arms and held me close. I noticed that I had smudged blood on his shoulder, staining his white T-shirt. The comfort of his hold was so wonderful that I hadn't even felt the pain in my chin. I was just three but for some reason was already hungry to be held and loved by a man. Grampie was comfortable being a loving father, and I would go back and stay with my beloved grandparents most of my childhood summers and even in my young-adult life. He was one of the only affectionate father figures in my early child-hood. Grampie always seemed to me a saint, and he awakened in me a longing to become a saint myself.

My father was a good and upright man. A hard-working mili-tary man and a new convert to the Catholic Church, he came from a broken family that had suffered generations of abandon-ment and rarely exhibited affection. Still, I was always proud of him. Although his work never interested me, I would listen to him talk about it because it meant that I had his attention. I took what I could get.

He adored my mother, but I often felt that I somehow inter-rupted their honeymoon. Too often I was told I should just be grateful that there's a roof he's providing, when all I wanted was to sit on his lap and be held.

My mother was a very good Catholic who devoted all her energies to stay-at-home motherhood. She raised us in the Faith, and she emphasized purity. That's why I knew the rules when it came to dating and boys, and I knew the rules about our Catholic Faith and never skipping Mass. From my earliest years, I feared hell and feared making a mistake. By the time I was four years old, I had already developed symptoms of OCD, depression, and strange addictions out of profound feelings of loneliness.

I ended up in a shrink's office by the time I was thirteen. He concluded that my behavior was most likely caused by sexual abuse. As I could not recall any sexual abuse, I concluded that I was either a freak or a huge sinner, or both. I felt that I was a failure and in danger of hell. My deep guilt aggravated my outsider status as a poor kid in a wealthy Catholic school. I truly didn't fit in anywhere. On Sundays, however, for one hour we were in a wonderful social setting in church; I felt ac-cepted by the parishioners and by God—even more than in my own home, and certainly more than in the world, where I felt like a reject.

At thirteen, I first smelled incense in church, during a Lenten week Adoration Mass. I heard words in a language I didn't know —Latin—in the moving hymn *"Tantum Ergo."* The Mass was breathtaking, the incense otherworldly. I stepped into a strange, beautiful realm where I was fully embraced. I had never experienced such transcendence before; it stayed with me, and awakened a longing that was good and holy.

Not long afterward, my mother spoke of healing the family tree and suggested that my addictions and other odd behaviors could be attacks that were spiritual in nature. Around that same time, we began saying the Rosary together. Soon after we started praying as a family, a recurring dream I had had since I was three and a half came to light: in it, a baby boy smiled at me from inside a toilet in the bathroom sink drain. My mother revealed that, unbeknownst to me, she had miscarried a baby at around the time those dreams started.

When I was a child, in my dreams I had been fascinated by "the boy in the toilet," but when I woke up, I had a strong fear of the bathroom in the dark. I was afraid the boy would come out of the drain. Soon, my mother had a Mass said for her miscarried baby at the cathedral in a special service for miscarried and aborted babies. She named him Mark William. In a matter weeks, my odd symptoms disappeared.

I became convinced that all my symptoms had, in fact, been somewhat spiritual in nature, combined with loneliness caused by longing for fatherly affection and a desire for more siblings. I believed my life would be marked by dedication to unborn babies. It was the early 1990s. I had just become aware of the meaning of abortion, and started teen pro-life groups in town.

I was off to what seemed like a decent start in my new Catholic high school. I got contact lenses, so I no longer had to look at people from behind hideously thick glasses that took up my whole face. When I was fifteen, I started to feel pretty, and my confidence and extroverted nature began to blossom.

When I was sixteen, I was allowed to date, and I dived at the opportunity. My longing from manly affection was desperate, but I knew the rules, so most of my early dating was largely innocent. I went from guy to guy to guy, getting free dinners and making out.

Then one weekend, after a teen youth retreat, I caught the eye of the bishop's altar server. He was outgoing and smooth, and went out with only the gorgeous girls, so when he made his move on me in the backseat of the packed car on the way home from the retreat, I was flattered and overcome by disbelief.

I thought, "Me?!"

Later, he brought me to his home. I was relaxed there. Whereas my home felt tense, his family was relaxed and spiritual at the same time. My parents trusted him, as did I. I was happy to hang out at his house.

He introduced me to alcohol. It took about thirty seconds for the Bud Light to kick in. Next thing you know, I was giggling and delighting in all the little compliments he and his friends were giving me. That's lame, I know, but it was *him*. He was the first guy I met who made me want to give him anything, even though I was committed to "saving myself for marriage."

My infatuation was brutally ended when he molested me while I was waking up after cuddling and spending the night with him (fully clothed). He apologized, but I took the blame myself, telling him it was "no biggie." I knew that he was already interested in the next girl.

That morning, the sky was gray over the Black Hills, and the sun appeared to be smaller than normal — just a gray ball behind the clouds. I went for a hike alone. I prayed, and I sobbed. I had lost much of my innocence, and I felt deep down that I wasn't good enough for him. I broke up with him, but I knew I was just doing it in order to be first to break up. Inside I was dying.

Graduation from high school freed me from wild parties and wilder boyfriends. I resolved to reform, and I got to know the folks who ran the Newman Center at the School of Mines and Technology in Rapid City.

The couple who ran it were Steubenville University graduates. They were young and hip but authentically good and holy. A young man named Tim Gray, also a Steubenville graduate, helped them out. I looked up to each of them as the kind of adult I wanted to be.

When our cathedral parish went to World Youth Day in 1993 to see Pope John Paul II, a friend and I spent much of the time talking with Tim, who accompanied our group as a chaperone. During that trip, I first saw apologetics in action, as my friend and I accompanied Tim through downtown Denver, where he evangelized even folks who are rabidly anti-Catholic. He spent hours talking to me and my friend about purity and chastity, and his words stayed with me as a challenge.

BYE, BYE, BOYS AND BOOZE

I was not convinced I could overcome my weakness for male affection and win the constant struggle to remain chaste, but he assured me I could. He encouraged me to get rid of all of my dark-metal CDs (I happened to be addicted to alternative music and mosh pits, including satanic music at the time), which I did right after returning from World Youth Day. I was resolved to stay holy.

When I was eighteen, the military transferred our family to England, which brings me back to the night the kind atheist family drove me to Mass. Although I returned home to my parents after that Mass, my heart was no longer obedient to them.

At the same time my younger brother was beginning to look for ways to leave home, and my younger sister kept mainly to herself or disappeared with her friends. When my parents traveled for three weeks to Germany for my father's heart surgery, they left us three teenagers on our own. There were to be no parties; and no one at all was to come into our home while they were gone. Those were the rules.

I promised I would abide by the rules, which I had no intention of keeping. Not only did I have a party; I also welcomed my atheist boyfriend into my room. We did not go all the way, but having a boy in my room was the next worst thing I could do in my parents' Catholic home — worse perhaps than our smoking marijuana out of the open window and giggling to our hearts' content. I had left behind the cheap Bud Light of my younger teens and had turned to more potent highs.

I gave little thought to my family, who were imperfect and yet loved me with a real love, and I opened my heart to that young, incredibly attractive, wealthy boy who was infatuated with me as if I were a goddess.

My parents quickly discovered the truth of what had transpired while they were away. They arranged to meet me at a nearby truck stop. The night was one of the darkest I've ever experienced. My military father laid down the law and its consequences. My mother was broken and sad, but submitted to my father's decision. All of us were brokenhearted, but I forged a wall; I played it cool. Fine.

They kicked me out of their home at the age of nineteen, in a foreign country.

I moved into a rented flat and finally felt free. My boyfriend stayed with me often. Because I was now convinced that my parents were more concerned with rules than with my heart, I came to see the Church as a hypocritical joke, filled with men and women who didn't in fact love. I felt like more of a liability to my parents than a human being, let alone their daughter. And so, my feeling of rejection led me gradually to ditch my Faith altogether and fling myself toward the young man and his family who showed me love and admiration.

I remember the day that I discovered that, strong-willed as I was, my resolve to partake in every sexual activity but actual intercourse was weakened by the smell of (unholy) incense blended with cheap stereo sounds in the background playing Pink Floyd music. I trusted my boyfriend, but he violated me fully. My shock blended with sobbing and defeat.

Once I was raped, I believed it was my fault and I despaired. I felt I was used goods, not worthy of even trying to return to church. I embraced the atheist mind-set and my boyfriend and his wealthy family. We went on exotic vacations, smoked countless quality joints, and indulged in endless hedonistic sex. I lost what few remnants of conscience I once had.

We went clubbing together at various clubs, but our favorite one was called the Coven. I had no idea at the time that a coven is a satanic reference, but I was drawn there—drawn to the drugs, drawn to the admiration of lustful men who thought my name and the fact that I was an American made me exotic. My pride grew, turning me fully to the world and away from the Creator.

Soon, relations with my boyfriend grew unsatisfactory. I started looking for other men while my boyfriend was busy at the club. I danced onstage, seeking to awaken more and more lust in my admirers, hoping to be satisfied by it. Technically, I remained faithful to my boyfriend, but I felt immoral. I thought I had nothing to lose and everything to gain.

Our parties increased, our days consumed with fun and the next "fix." For the first time in my life, I was truly popular, the girlfriend of a well-respected and wealthy medical student; the girl who was noticed, and the one who was even finally respected and admired by a family. The pleasure was indescribable, and it seemed that a path of roses and bliss awaited me, growing ever larger and more abundant. It seemed like heaven on earth.

One morning, we were all offhandedly discussing abortion, and I discovered that his mother had helped assist in one. I remember her words, "Well, of course, I think it's a good idea! I mean, we don't want any cyclopses coming into the world, do we?" Apparently, abortion was for babies with disabilities.

Everyone laughed. I said nothing but felt a tug on my stifled conscience. *Shal, how far have you come? Are you not even pro-life anymore?* For my whole life, I had believed in the sacredness of unborn life. Had I become indifferent? Did I care about anyone or anything anymore?

I soon learned that my boyfriend had to move to another city to pursue his medical career in college, and I couldn't follow. Because his parents wanted to ensure that he would not sacrifice his medical career for his infatuation with me, they suddenly turned on me, telling me to stay away. He didn't come this far not to become a doctor, and I'd better not try to convince him otherwise. They forbade us to see each other.

Once again, I was betrayed. I was alone, in my empty flat, staring at pathetic soap operas and MTV after work; and very, very lonely. My depression was like none I had ever experienced. I was not only alone, but I was separated from my family and from God.

I returned to the Coven, content now to bring almost anyone back to my flat. I was already lost. What did it matter? And so there were many mornings I would wake up with someone in my bed whom I didn't remember bringing home the night before. I remember beginning to miss my boyfriend, so I visited him at his Oxford campus. I stayed with him for several weekends. He seemed truly to miss me, and I began to plan how we could join our lives. I applied to an Oxford college and was accepted.

BYE, BYE, BOYS AND BOOZE

Until the new semester started, I had always to return to my flat in the small town not far from my parents' house—parents whom I rarely saw.

In her charity, my mother took me to London for my twenty-first birthday. At the suggestion of the priest who had been my pastor, we visited a cloistered convent. I sat there, before a huge monstrance, feeling as if I were sitting on spikes. I had loved Adoration and Mass as a child, but now I became uncomfortable, either bored and restless or waiting for some sort of lightning bolt to hit me. I said a Hail Mary but didn't mean a word of it. I couldn't wait to get out of there. For His part, God Himself in the Host within the monstrance was staring right at me and beginning to sear a hole through the walls I built.

As for me, I was looking forward to a huge party that night with my Oxford friends and my boyfriend. I couldn't wait to be drunk and high and spoiled with attention by them all. It was the grandest party of my life. And then, of course, my boyfriend returned to his university and I to my lonely flat, where I even tried to flirt with the landlord. I knew it would all be better once I started at the university in Oxford and could join my boyfriend for good. I just needed to get away from that silly little town and the silence of my family.

I'm a down-to-earth person, not given to voices or visions. I even struggle to believe in apparitions. After the Resurrection, I would most likely have been like St. Thomas. Nonetheless, one night at midnight I suddenly burst awake and sat straight up, gasping for air. Then I heard it, clear as day, in my mind: "If you continue as you are, you will go to hell."

I began to sob.

Uncontrollably.

How could I even begin to change?

I still had in my room a crucifix, which I had kept for sentimentality, and I stared at it. I realized that I had become a slave to my passions and could not free myself. I could not turn away from my boyfriend or my addictions, and I knew it.

So I tried to stare down the cross, and said, sobbing, "Okay, *You* are going to have to free me. I can't." On a tiny piece of paper, which I taped behind the cross, I wrote a note that simply said, "Save me."

And I let it be.

But I was shaken.

Softly at first, in my mind I began to "hear" the words "Go. Go back to America." Gradually, the voice came to occupy all my thoughts. I tried to ignore the command, but it got louder and louder, almost deafening and urgent. "Go. Go!"

But what would I do there?

I had barely any money and no idea where I would go. I knew that I had always wanted to be a missionary, so I contacted a Catholic volunteer group in my home state of Florida. They accepted only applicants with a bachelor's degree, but the leader of the group agreed to interview me in Orlando.

My parents were pleased with my decision, and even more pleased that I was returning to the Faith. I moved back in with them for the last three weeks I was in England. We reconciled, and had a beautiful Christmas together. I made a full confession to our dear priest at Immaculate Conception Church in the little town near Oxford, and for the first time in years, I was at peace, indescribable peace.

Of course, my boyfriend and my atheist friends could not comprehend my actions; I could barely comprehend them myself, except that there was a constant command of "Go!" in my mind that I could not shake. It's hard to explain to those who do not believe in God that "God told me I needed to move." I must have sounded like a lunatic. Given the risk, the move could possibly have been quite foolish.

And the peace ... It was better than all the earthly pleasures I had ever experienced. It all flooded back into my heart and soul: all those words of confidence that people like Tim Gray had taught me years earlier, the comforting prayers my mother and grandparents taught me, the smell of holy incense....

I got on that plane with fifty dollars in my pocket, leaving all other earthly goods behind. It was the biggest risk I had ever taken. If I wasn't accepted, I would be homeless and alone.

But I was strangely at peace.

For the first week I was in Florida awaiting the results of my interview, I returned by myself each evening to an empty trailer that someone had donated for the volunteers. I lay in a fetal position, sobbing, alone, while I withdrew from many addictions, with no one to comfort me, and unfathomable pain and loneliness.

Although I did not have a bachelor's degree, somehow they accepted me. I was overjoyed, and excited to find out where I would be placed as a full-time missionary. I could choose from five sites in different parts of Florida.

The first site I visited was L'Arche Harbor House in Jacksonville. This is a community comprising four homes serving mentally and physically disabled adults. I arrived at the front door of the main house with no idea of what to expect, still withdrawing from my former lifestyle, still wondering what on earth I was doing. I was greeted by a gentleman named Scotty, with Down syndrome. He opened the door and, without saying a word, walked up and hugged me. There were no judgments, no words, nothing fancy—just a hug that still brings tears to my eyes whenever I remember it. I melted on Scotty's shoulder and began to cry.

I was home.

Just one month later, I would meet Corey, my future husband, a Navy pilot who occasionally volunteered at the community. I was fully converted back into the Catholic Church, and Corey and I soon became friends. At one point, we both joked that we hoped to have ten kids one day. We both laughed, and I thought "Whoa! How many guys want to have that many kids?" I tried to date other guys, but I was still failing, it seemed, to find anyone who was remotely "marriage material."

It was time to give my dating life over to God. And so, on my lunch break, I went downtown to the cathedral in Jacksonville to my first daily Mass in years. During the Consecration, I sighed inwardly out of pure frustration and practically yelled at God: "Okay! You take this! You can have my dating life! I'm fine being single or even a nun!" Corey was at that same Mass, and we happened to see each other. We went to lunch at a Jewish restaurant and ate what I didn't know then was wedding soup. Three months later we were engaged.

On the day of our wedding, Corey and I were surrounded by both our families as well as our community from L'Arche. In the same beautiful Cathedral of the Immaculate Conception in

Jacksonville, where we ran into each other before our first real date, we were married by the priest from Immaculate Conception Church in England. Watching the L'Arche residents dance to the oldies with no inhibitions was one of the greatest memories we have of our reception.

In the first year of our marriage, Corey and I faced infertility as well as other deep crosses. Then, just as God surprised me with life in Him by calling me back to the Church, so he healed my infertility and has given us ten beautiful children.

After years of prayer and family healing, my dad is now a dear friend of mine. He even graduated from the Augustine Institute in Denver, a school that was formed by none other than Dr. Tim Gray, the young friend from my teens. My beautiful mother continues to be a holy witness of long-suffering faith and gentle love, and my siblings are godly witnesses with incredible personalities and gifts. We've had much healing in my family. I'm grateful to the many people God put into my life at perfect times, even those who caused pain and challenges. Even in difficult times, God used them to guide me and my family to exactly where He wants us.

Over the years, especially in the last decade, we have experienced intense struggles and unbearable pain, and uncounted mysteries that have yet to be understood. But even more, life has given us surprises — good surprises, whenever I've put my trust in life's Author.

Sometimes, death and destruction seemed to surround me like so many lions, yet I have found that if I simply cling to the One who has looked out for me from the beginning — no matter how I've turned away from Him — He will continue to surprise me with His life. When I surrender to Him, He puts me into amazing circumstances and incredible relationships I could never have expected.

If He has shown me such mercy, with all my errors and vices, He certainly will embrace you, no matter what your circumstances are. As people, we will fail each other; and none of us can fully fill the empty space in each of our hearts. But there is someone who can fill that empty space. Ultimately, He is the one who scooped me up and cuddles me on His divine shoulder, even if my chin is bleeding all over it. Life is an incredible adventure.

SHALIMAR MASTERS lives in rural Ohio with her husband and ten children. She loves British tea, icons, watching Amish buggies navigate the roads, raising her children, and, most of all, her faith and love for Christ the Bridegroom.

LIFEVICTORIOUS.COM

SHALIMAMMA@GMAIL.COM

PAINFUL LESSONS OF THE HEART

LISA DUFFY

"You look sick. Are you all right?" the woman next to me whispered. I nodded with an appreciative look, but I lied. I felt as if I had just crawled out of the grave. The priest who was giving a talk to our group of Catholic women shot us an irritated look, as if to say, "This is a *silent* retreat!"

This was only my second day on the weeklong retreat, and I was seriously doubting I would be able to make it to the end. There was a volcano brewing in my stomach and a faint dizziness that made the nausea worse, but I was determined to power through it and stay until the final day.

Where had I picked up this stomach flu? The airport? The taxi ride? I don't know, but it was definitely bad news. When Father's talk was over, we all took a break, and I retreated to the comfort of my tiny room. As I lay on the bed, I drifted off to sleep dreaming of my husband, who was far away in Atlanta.

Jim was my second husband, and we had gotten married just one month before this retreat took place. Eight years earlier, if you had told me I would be on such a retreat, I would have laughed. I had been through a very bitter and messy divorce, and my world was steeped in hurt and anger—much of which I blamed on God.

A retreat?

Spending time with God?

Not a chance!

I'm a cradle Catholic. When I married at age twenty-six, I married for life. I invested in my marriage all my hopes and dreams of raising a large, happy Catholic family, just like the one I had grown up in: solid parents and seven siblings.

Truth be told, I did a rather poor job of selecting a spouse, and an even worse job of recognizing the warning signs that were obvious during our engagement—signs that spoke of a relationship in trouble from the start. The priest who conducted the little bit of marriage preparation we received didn't bat an eye that fateful day R. and I approached the altar, so we were married in January 1990.

Four years later, R. walked out, never to return.

By then, I had lost three children to miscarriages, each of which broke my heart. The first miscarriage occurred at twelve weeks and my OB/GYN, Dr. Sanford, simply chalked it up to the fact that many women lose their first baby to miscarriage. "That's what happens sometimes, and it's not your fault," he assured me. It was a very sad time. I never had the privilege of holding that baby in my arms, and it was hard to get over that loss. Still, I was consoled by the fact that we could try again and likely be successful.

The second miscarriage took place at fourteen weeks. During our scheduled sonogram, we were told that there was no heartbeat. Dr. Sanford was one of the best in his field and had seen thousands of cases like mine. He offered some reasons why this might have happened again, but frankly, I didn't really hear much of what he said. I was so disappointed and so sad.

"It's not your fault. There was nothing you could have done to prevent this from happening," came the words once more. I was grateful for his compassion, but the only thing that could bring me consolation at that point would have been having my two lost babies there with me.

These miscarriages left me anxious and consumed by worry. *Would I ever be able to carry a child to term? How many babies would I have to lose before one lived?* I mentioned my concerns to Dr. Sanford, who said we should explore what might be causing the miscarriages. In the months that followed, he ran some tests to rule out possible culprits such as lupus and endometriosis. Every test came back negative. With each result, I gained more hope that a third pregnancy would be the charm.

In mid-September, we received the news that I was eight weeks pregnant, and with cautious excitement I made the announcement to family and friends. R., however, didn't seem excited. He didn't really even seem that interested, but I had enough enthusiasm for everyone, so as the weeks proceeded, I began picking out names and buying baby clothes.

One day, without warning, I began to bleed profusely. Alarmed, I called Dr. Sanford, who saw me right away. He admitted that he had no idea why this was happening. I was not in any pain, and a sonogram revealed a strong heartbeat, so he put me on bed rest until the bleeding stopped.

But it never did.

The weeks progressed, and I followed Dr. Sanford's directives to the letter, but the bleeding remained constant. I prayed Rosary after Rosary, hoping things would be okay, but in my heart, there was a growing despair and a deepening resentment toward God. This likely made my prayers sound less like fervent, humble requests, and more like a spoiled child stomping her foot in front of her father, demanding to have things her way. Then, in early December there was a major breakthrough that would reveal the answers we were so desperately seeking.

I went in for my normally scheduled sonogram. I was eighteen weeks along, and my uterus had expanded to the point that made the problem causing the bleeding obvious. I had what is medically referred to as a bicornuate uterus, or simply put, a heartlike uterus. There were two compartments within one uterus. The baby was growing in one side and the other side was "confused," as Dr. Sanford explained, so its response was to bleed.

There were no medications I could take that would remedy this situation, and there was no cause for any type of intervention. My orders were to go home and proceed exactly as I had been doing: strict bed rest and no stress.

PAINFUL LESSONS OF THE HEART

A week later, I woke up feeling as if I had been hit by a semitruck. R. was at work, and I spent the day in bed feeling miserable. By the time he got home, I was lying on the floor with a high fever, moaning in pain. He rushed me to the hospital.

My temperature was 106 degrees, and I was in labor. After an excruciatingly painful examination, the ER doctors informed me the bleeding had caused a major infection, which had taken the baby's life and caused me to go into labor. They feared the infection would take me, too.

Suddenly there were doctors shouting orders and nurses running frantically. It was, in some ways, an out-of-body experience. I could hear myself wailing in pain as I lay on the gurney waiting for surgery to begin, begging anyone who could hear me for water to drink, but with the prick of a needle, anesthesia flooded my veins, and it all faded away.

Hours later, a rude awakening.

I opened my eyes and saw blurry shapes come into focus. A short, stocky Portuguese nurse was calling my name. "Leeeeeza! It's time to wake up, Leeza!" I coughed and felt as if I'd been punched in the chest. Tubes had been inserted in my lungs during the surgery to keep me breathing and left me feeling very sore. The nurse wrapped me in warm blankets and kept calling my name, but I closed my eyes. I knew my baby was gone.

One year later, life had become quite difficult and my relationships with the two most important people in my life, God and my husband, were strained at best. When I went to Sunday Mass, all I could think was: "Why, God? Why are you doing this?" I sat alone in the pew, trying hard to ignore the babies and the young children and focus on the Mass, but it took all my energy to concentrate.

By this point, R. had stopped going to Mass with me and had, in fact, stopped practicing his Faith. Much to my dismay, he had turned into someone I hardly recognized, able to make me feel terrible in five words or less, particularly about my life as a Catholic.

His words hurt, but I refused to give up, hoping and praying that things would change and our lives together would get better. Despite the challenges we faced, I loved him and I had committed myself to him, so I was in it for better or for worse. Still, resentment in my heart kept growing.

Then Dr. Sanford told me about groundbreaking surgery for which I was a perfect candidate. The new procedure made it possible for him and his team to reconstruct my uterus so I could carry a child to term. There were risks involved, but since I was unwilling to take artificial contraception to prevent future pregnancies, he recommended I consider this surgery.

In April 1992, I was admitted to Cedars Sinai Hospital for the procedure. The surgery was a success. I had a brand new, perfectly shaped, one-room uterus in which there was plenty of room for a baby to grow. Unfortunately, the surgery inadvertently rendered me sterile.

Dr. Sanford said that the odds of my ever conceiving a child were now less than 1 percent. "But," he added, "with all the advancements in the field of in vitro fertilization and other kinds of infertility treatment, you'll soon have much better odds. It might take several years, but if you're willing to try, something might work." In vitro fertilization was not an option for me because of my Catholic values, so at that point, I just gave up hope. I went back to my everyday routine, feeling heartbroken and angry.

Where was God? I thought He was in favor of growing a family? How could He let this happen to me?

R. was distant. I tried to talk to him about the miscarriages, partially to see how they impacted him, partially to strengthen our marriage by sharing our grief together, but he just wasn't interested. He began working late and disappearing for hours on the weekends without a reasonable explanation. One Sunday afternoon after being gone all night without calling, R. came home and told me he wanted a divorce.

For years I struggled with these losses: my three babies and then R.'s sudden departure. I've tried many times to describe what that period of my life was like: wandering in an endless desert, trying to find the light switch in a room that was pitch-black, sinking into a pit of quicksand with no one to help me out. Although those analogies come close, nothing can really articulate what I was going through. At thirty years old, I was divorced, childless, without hope of ever having children, and Catholic. Not a great combination.

I've often wondered why God allows miscarriages. Not in a "why does God allow evil" kind of way: God's ways are not our ways, and we won't understand the many tragedies that happen in this life until we die and can ask Him.

But it is difficult for me to make sense out of miscarriages in particular. God breathes life into beautiful, tiny souls and then calls them home before they've had a chance to really live.

Why does He do that?

During my first six months alone, trying to adjust to my new normal, the shock and numbness I felt began to fade and give way to anger and bitterness. I was angry that God had allowed the failure of the one thing that should have lasted a lifetime: my marriage. The reality was, however, that the poor choices I had made were the primary reason my marriage failed. But the powerful emotions I experienced blinded me from recognizing this early on. It would take some time for me to learn to accept responsibility for the decisions I had made. In the meantime, I was at war with God.

Many women who suffer miscarriages today are much more graceful in the way they handle their losses. They give their unborn children names and sometimes hold funeral services for them. I think this is beautiful. Back when it happened to me, however, I'd never heard of such things so I had never done them, especially because I never knew the gender of my children, not even the one I carried to eighteen weeks. In my heart, I believe I had two boys and a girl, but I will never know until, God willing, I meet them in heaven.

PAINFUL LESSONS OF THE HEART

Trying to put a positive spin on the loss of a child through miscarriage, people often say things like "God needed another angel" or some other well-intended but discomforting remark, and I heard that many times. Unfortunately, such comments just exacerbate the pain of the loss. Losing a third child compounded my sorrow, and I gave up on God.

I had no spiritual life during my first year after the divorce. Sure, I did a lot of tearful pleading and begging God in those first few days, and, no doubt, that was one form of praying, but as the shock began to wear off and anger set in, my ability and desire to pray went right out the window. My sorrow was too deep, and I just couldn't find any words to say to God.

I never stopped going to Mass, but I did so only out of obligation because attending was a painful experience. I noticed all the families that seemed perfect and happy. They were reminders of what I had lost. So I would show up late and leave early, making sure I just put in my required time.

Everyday life was like wandering through a battlefield with me one of the walking wounded. When I thought about the future, I saw nothing good, especially not my dream of motherhood. Sorrow and anger consumed me, tossing me about like a little toy on the ocean. The pain seemed insurmountable. Anger and despair were my constant companions.

Fast forward two and a half years. I had a new life, a new home, a successful career, an exciting social life: I was a totally different person … and desperately unhappy. I had sought happiness and healing in the world, plunging with abandon into what I call the "culture of divorce." Judged by the standards of everyone I knew, I should have been happy, but, in fact, I was well on my way to becoming a bitter, cynical alcoholic who would be incapable of having a successful relationship with anyone.

One day as I stood in front of my mirror and got dressed for work, I found it impossible to look myself in the eye. I could barely apply my makeup. I knew I was far away from God, and even further away from being the woman He had created me to be. I was ashamed, even though all my friends at that time would have told me I was foolish.

Then, I had yet another frightening thought, which forced me to look at myself in the mirror. I realized that if I met the right man for me, he wouldn't recognize me as the right one for him.

I was that lost!

When a person comes out of a failed marriage, it's almost as if a carnival barker were suddenly calling her to come play the games and ride the rides. *Escape your troubles and forget your cares! Anything goes now because you are free!* There's always someone there egging you on, fixing you up with someone she knows, encouraging you to let go of your Catholic guilt and be happy. This is the "culture of divorce," and I embraced it fully. I played the games and rode the rides, never realizing that the true love I was seeking was becoming less and less possible.

What I needed were words of wisdom to wake me up and set me back on the right track—words such as those of Pope St. John Paul II in his book *Love and Responsibility*:

> Man's capacity for love depends on his willingness
> consciously to seek a good together with others, and to
> subordinate himself to that good for the sake of others,
> or to others for the sake of that good. Love is exclusively
> the portion of human persons.[3]

It was unfortunate that I would not read these beautiful words
until much later. Nothing in my life at this time reflected this
image of love. Although I felt the tug of love many times, I was
not doing the things I did for the good of anyone else; I was in it
to make myself feel better. I wanted an end to my pain and suffering. I was not a *lover* in John Paul's sense of the word at all; I had
become a *user*. There was no giving for the sake of others; there
was only taking and using others for my own self-gratification.
This is where my intense guilt came from.

And so, I wrestled with my conscience.

On the one hand, my divorce had me fairly convinced
that the Catholic standards that I had been raised with were
unrealistic. The bar had been set too high. How could I have
been so naïve to think that marriage could be permanent and
exclusive?

On the other hand, most of my family members had stable,
happy marriages, which contradicted my growing cynicism.

I just couldn't find the balance.

But it was precisely that image of real love — selfless love
that becomes a gift — that would ultimately win my heart and
bring me back to God.

---

[3]   Karol Wojtyla/John Paul II, *Love and Responsibility* (San
Francisco: Ignatius Press, 1993), 29.

So on that morning as I stood before myself in the mirror, ashamed and deeply saddened at what I had become, God's grace penetrated my heart and breathed life back into it.

I felt His mercy, and I felt His love almost as if He were holding me close to Him. I came to the hard realization that the truths I had rejected about real love, selfless love, and God's plan for marriage—truths that could be found only in my Catholic Faith—would not be my downfall; they would be my life preserver. Practicing love as giving a gift, not using others for my gain, would be the light to illuminate my way forward and give me hope for my future.

I was filled with a powerful motivation to change my life and to begin that very moment. Suddenly, after years of silence, I had words to say to God, and they flowed from my heart as rapidly and forcefully as Niagara Falls. "I'm so sorry. Please don't give up on me. I want to change."

And change I did.

I went to Confession.

I didn't stand in line on a Saturday; I made an appointment with a priest so I could make a general confession. The day before the appointment, I had just about talked myself out of going because I knew I would feel humiliated by admitting all my sins.

My heart was heavy with the weight of my divorce, the loss of my children, and all my poor choices. Yet I forced myself to go. There was a driving determination to overcome all the many obstacles with which I had willfully littered my path. I needed to raise the bar on my own standards and tackle every problem until I was back on track.

As I sat in Fr. Joe's office that day, I experienced floodgates opening. Everything that had happened since my husband left came rushing out. I didn't know how to stop it.

I cried.

I told him how abandoned I felt, not just by my husband, but by God. It felt so good to be able to admit the truth.

When I was finished, Fr. Joe replied, "Lisa, you say you've felt abandoned by God, but it seems He's had His hand on your shoulder the whole time. God didn't abandon you; He's been with you the entire way."

No words could have been more healing.

I felt a burden lifted from me and a great sense of consolation. After some wise spiritual direction, Fr. Joe gave me absolution, and I walked away from that confession experiencing the peace I had been looking for all along.

That confession cemented my belief that only through my Faith and the sacraments would I ever find real healing.

But I had another hard lesson to learn.

As long as I refused to take responsibility for my contributions to the failure of my marriage, I would always blame my ex-spouse for what happened. As long as I blamed him for my problems and held tight to my anger toward God, I would remain a victim. As long as I was a victim, I would remain stuck in despair and never be able to move forward to the happy life God had waiting for me.

I had to break this vicious cycle, and for me, that meant continuing to take real, concrete steps toward eliminating the obstacles that were in my way.

With that, my next step was to apply for an annulment. At times, it was very difficult — particularly the lengthy questionnaire with all its probing questions. It's tough to revisit painful memories and dredge up things deliberately forgotten, but there's great wisdom in completing this exercise because there's a cleansing aspect to it all.

Taking that step, it turns out, was liberating. I matured emotionally. To my surprise, rolling up my sleeves and digging through the dirt was therapeutic. It helped me pluck out those ugly weeds of blame and resentment, leaving fertile soil in which God could plant His grace and mercy.

On a warm June day in 1997, I opened my mailbox and saw there a letter from the archdiocese. It carried the decision about my annulment application; it would determine my new direction in life.

Would it announce that my marriage was indeed valid, and I was bound to my ex-spouse until one of us died? Or would it declare that there was never a valid bond and I was free to marry again in the Church?

I stared at it for a minute before I reached in. I was stressed out and relieved all at the same time because, although I had waited two years for this day to come, I knew the decision would change the rest of my life.

Several minutes later, I stared out my kitchen window with a bittersweet feeling. The archdiocese declared that I never had a valid marriage bond, and I was free to marry again in the Church.

It was not a "jump for joy" moment because I never wanted divorce in the first place. But there was a great sense of relief and a soothing, healing feeling.

That terrible period in my life had ended. I had the closure I needed and a firm direction to head in. Now I could move forward as a whole person.

Fast-forward several years, and I was truly a new person. I had made a lot of changes and experienced great personal growth. I was happy again, and much of that happiness came from repairing my relationship with God. I realized that my self-worth was rooted in Him, not in what happened to me or in what people thought of me.

For a brief period, I discerned a vocation to the religious life after wondering whether the fact that my marriage failed, I had lost my children, and I was now sterile was God's way of telling me I was supposed to be a nun all along.

God had a different plan.

On a rare warm Connecticut day in April of 1999, the door to my office opened and an associate walked in with Jim, a new hire. Jim and I started out working together and soon became friends. It was a great beginning for our relationship. In November 1999 we began dating, and the following Valentine's Day he proposed, knowing we would never have children of our own, that it would be adoption or nothing. In June 2000 we were married, and I felt I had finally come full circle in my life.

I was finally home.

So here I was just a month after our marriage on the second day of a weeklong silent retreat, far away from Jim and wishing I could be with him, or, more accurately, wishing he could take care of me because I felt so bad. I lay on the bed in my tiny room at the retreat house turning green from nausea, when a thought struck me like a bolt of lightning.

I was incredulous, but I knew without a doubt it was morning sickness, which meant ... *I was pregnant!*

I wanted to jump up and run out to tell the other women — one of whom was my new mother-in-law — but I couldn't. It was a silent retreat.

And then it dawned on me, the sneaky brilliance of what God was doing. It almost felt deliberate that He was the only one I could share my joy with for the next four days. I lay back down on the bed and stared at the ceiling, saying prayers of thanksgiving and joy with tears streaming down my face.

It was obvious to me that God wanted me fully to comprehend and appreciate the miracle he had brought about, and how great His love for me was. Despite all the losses, the heartache, and the diagnosis of sterilization, I was going to have a baby!

A week or so later, I visited my OB/GYN for the standard blood work and examination. Afterward, as I sat in her office, she said to me, "I hope you realize what a miracle this is, Lisa. Someone with your history should not be able to get pregnant."

She didn't have to tell me; I knew that better than anyone. God does what He wants, and in my life He wanted children.

As I write this chapter, Jim and I are celebrating seventeen years of marriage, and we have three healthy, happy teenagers, each one twenty-one months apart. They are the joy of our lives.

In the end, the world doesn't bring us happiness: it comes from God's love for us and from His design for living. The teachings of the Catholic Faith bring the greatest happiness, especially understanding that true love is selfless.

With God, all things are possible, even after divorce and miscarriages, and "all things work for good for those who love God" (Rom. 8:28).

There is no greater joy than experiencing His love in action.

LISA DUFFY is a Catholic author and speaker with more than twenty years of experience in helping people rebuild their lives after divorce. The author of several books, including *A Road to Healing: Daily Reflections for Divorced Catholics*, she has also instituted the Journey of Hope parish program in parishes across the United States and in Canada. She contributes to many print and online publications, such as Aleteia.org. Aside from her dedication to her family, Lisa speaks at conferences, appears on television and radio, and coaches one-on-one and in groups.

LISA@LISADUFFY.COM

LISADUFFY.COM

Sophia Institute

Sophia Institute is a nonprofit institution that seeks to nurture the spiritual, moral, and cultural life of souls and to spread the Gospel of Christ in conformity with the authentic teachings of the Roman Catholic Church.

Sophia Institute Press fulfills this mission by offering translations, reprints, and new publications that afford readers a rich source of the enduring wisdom of mankind.

Sophia Institute also operates two popular online Catholic resources: CrisisMagazine.com and CatholicExchange.com.

Crisis Magazine provides insightful cultural analysis that arms readers with the arguments necessary for navigating the ideological and theological minefields of the day. *Catholic Exchange* provides world news from a Catholic perspective as well as daily devotionals and articles that will help you to grow in holiness and live a life consistent with the teachings of the Church.

In 2013, Sophia Institute launched Sophia Institute for Teachers to renew and rebuild Catholic culture through service to Catholic education. With the goal of nurturing the spiritual, moral, and cultural life of souls, and an abiding respect for the role and work of teachers, we strive to provide materials and programs that are at once enlightening to the mind and ennobling to the heart; faithful and complete, as well as useful and practical.

Sophia Institute gratefully recognizes the Solidarity Association for preserving and encouraging the growth of our apostolate over the course of many years. Without their generous and timely support, this book would not be in your hands.

www.SophiaInstitute.com
www.CatholicExchange.com
www.CrisisMagazine.com
www.SophiaInstituteforTeachers.org

Sophia Institute Press® is a registered trademark of Sophia Institute. Sophia Institute is a tax-exempt institution as defined by the Internal Revenue Code, Section 501(c)(3). Tax I.D. 22-2548708.